EASY
INDIAN
COOKBOOK

EASY
INDIAN
COOKBOOK

MANJU MALHI

THE STEP-BY-STEP GUIDE TO DELICIOUSLY EASY INDIAN FOOD AT HOME

DUNCAN BAIRD PUBLISHERS

LONDON

Easy Indian Cookbook
Manju Malhi

This edition first published in the United Kingdom and Ireland in 2015
by DBP, an imprint of Watkins Media Limited
19 Cecil Court
London WC2N 4EZ

Managing Editor: Grace Cheetham
Editors: Beverly Le Blanc and Nicole Bator
Managing Designer: Manisha Patel
Designers: Luana Gobbo and Saskia Janssen
Studio Photography: William Lingwood
Photography Assistant: Kate Malone
Stylists: Jennifer White (food) and Helen Trent (props)

British Library Cataloguing-in-Publication Data:
A CIP record for this book is available from the British Library

ISBN: 978-1-84483-894-3

10 9 8 7 6 5 4 3 2

Typeset in Spectrum and Univers
Colour reproduction by Scanhouse, Malaysia
Printed in China

Author's acknowledgments

A big thank you to my mum Kami, Meno Malhi, Khazina, Werner Van
Peppen, Pauline Barrett, Robin Barrett, Jo and Nicholas Barrett, Louise
Robins, Juliana Barclay, Aruna Sood, Abha and Bill Adams, Sean Adams,
Girja Shanker Vohra, Monica Narula, Jeni Barnett, Alan Coxon, Paul
Hollywood, John Humphrys, Antony Worrall Thompson, Sonu Verma,
Sunita Verma, Puneet Gautam, Akshay Choubey, Seema Chandra, James
Macconachie, Stephanie Gerra, Rob Butler, Sam West, Robbie Sims, Matt
Barnard, James Shovlin, Tim Hughes, Laura Bootham, Nicola Phoenix,
Sudha Kaviraj, Neely Sood, Nik Gulhane, Matt and Kelly Brito, Leona
Daly, Simon Wain, Natasha Page, Liam Hamilton, Sophie Hillwood-Harris,
Caroline Blackadder, Dave Baker, Ben Robinson, Chris Kirby, Sanjay
Austa, Sona Sareen, Ceramica Blue and Books for Cooks.

Publisher's note

While every care has been taken in compiling the recipes for this book,
Watkins Media Limited, or any other persons who have been involved in
working on this publication, cannot accept responsibility for any errors or
omissions, inadvertent or not, that may be found in the recipes or text,
nor for any problems that may arise as a result of preparing one of these
recipes. If you are pregnant or breastfeeding or have any special dietary
requirements or medical conditions, it is advisable to consult a medical
professional before following any of the recipes contained in this book.

Notes on the recipes

Unless otherwise stated:
• Use fresh herbs and chillies
• Do not mix metric and imperial measurements
• 1 tsp = 5ml
  1 tbsp = 15ml
  1 cup = 250ml

CONTENTS

INTRODUCTION

It's little wonder that we are drawn to the cuisine of India: everything about it awakens the senses – sensuous aromas, vibrant colours and fabulous textures are present in every element, from the smoothest, palest grain of rice to the intense crimson of delicate saffron threads. Indian cuisine is perfume for the nose, relish for the lips, nourishment for the body and nectar for the soul.

India's one billion people eat what is naturally and seasonally available. Influenced by geography and climate, many religions and languages, and centuries of history, the country's 31 states boast a dizzying array of cuisines and specialities reflective of each region's character. In North India, the food is rich, with plenty of cream and warming spices to protect against the severe winters. In the extreme heat of the south, some of India's hottest and most exotic dishes feature fresh or green spices, which help to cool the body. Western India has embraced the most diverse and cosmopolitan global food trends, while to the east, where the Bengali and Assamese styles of cuisine are most prevalent, simplicity is key.

Given such diversity, it is ironic that when the rest of the world thinks of Indian food, curry is the first thing that springs to mind. In fact, although what we call curry is now recognized internationally, the term – originally coined by the British to describe the thousands of different stews and soups that shared common ingredients such as turmeric, cumin, garlic, ginger and chillies – is rarely used in India.

What unifies the cooking of this vast country, first and foremost, is not the use of "curry powder", as many believe, but rather a reliance on many spices and the ability to draw out and balance all of their distinctive flavours and aromas. Indian cooks are adept at concocting their own spice blends to season savoury dishes. *Garam masala*, which literally means a mixture of hot spices, is the most common, and every household will have its own special, signature combination. Chillies also appear frequently, but it is a common misconception that all Indian food is hot. Once you understand that the heat of a dish depends solely upon on the amount of chilli contained in it, you can easily adjust the intensity of a dish to suit your palette.

Dishes develop and change as a result of many factors. In India, certain foods are reserved for special occasions or festivals; others are taboo in some situations. Religion plays its part as well: Muslims do not eat pork because the pig is deemed unhygienic, and Hindus do not consume beef because the cow is considered sacred. The Hindu vegetarian tradition is widespread in India, yet many Hindus do eat meat. Furthermore, many of the dishes we think of as traditionally Indian actually sprang to life in the West. For example, Chicken Tikka Masala (see page 84) is one of the most popular curries outside India – but it was invented in British kitchens by Bangladeshi restaurateurs.

This book balances all of these influences, contrasts and contradictions with the many similarities that characterize and unify Indian cookery. With recipes from every part of the country, along with some of the most popular restaurant inventions from the West, it is your guide to exploring, demystifying and creating delicious, mouthwatering Indian meals that you will be proud to share with your friends and family.

PART 1

THE BASICS

Food without **spices** *is like summer without sunshine – and this is very much the ethos of Indian* **cooking***. First-time cooks often find the number of spices and ingredients used in Indian cuisine to be quite daunting – but the* **simple** *truth is that preparing an Indian meal is very* **straightforward***. Mastering just a few basic techniques and becoming familiar with some of the* **essential** *ingredients will strip away the* **mystery** *and make preparing Indian food less time-consuming, much more satisfying and incredibly* **rewarding***.*

    Discover how to make **delicious** *chutneys, relishes and pickles to add layers of flavour to your* **home-cooked** *meals. Then move on to cooking with spices – by far the most important skill in Indian cookery. Begin by dry-roasting and* **frying** *spices, then* **creating** *flavourful spice blends. Breadmaking may be considered an art form by some, but with a little practice you'll be surprised at how* **easy** *Indian* **breads** *such as naans and chapatis are to make. Finally, learn the basic methods for preparing* **traditional** *Indian rice dishes, from Plain Basmati Rice to Saffron Rice and Tamarind Rice. Once you* **master** *the recipes in this chapter, you'll be on your way to opening a whole new world of Indian delights the* **authentic** *way.*

INGREDIENTS

DAIRY

Clarified butter (ghee) – *Ghee* is evaporated and clarified butter made from cow's or buffalo's milk. The butter is melted and then simmered long enough to boil off all the water, during which time it develops a nutty taste. Although not a real substitute, normal butter comes close. However, ghee is available in supermarkets.

Paneer (paneer) – *Paneer* is the most common Indian cheese. Unlike most cheeses, it does not melt when cooked and it contains no salt. It is an important source of protein for vegetarians and is used in both sweet and savoury dishes.

Yogurt (dahi) – An essential ingredient in Indian cooking, yogurt is a staple for many vegetarians and many homes in India still make their own practically every day. There are countless uses for yogurt but the main ones are making yogurt drinks and chutneys, such as raitas, and using yogurt as a souring agent, a thickening agent, a meat tenderizer and a flavour enhancer. The yogurt in India comes from buffalo's milk and is thick and rich. Greek-style yogurt and natural unsweetened yogurt are the nearest substitutes.

FRUIT AND VEGETABLES

Coconut (nariyal) – One of the most important ingredients in southern, western and eastern vegetarian cooking is coconut. It is sliced, grated or used in liquid form.

To prepare fresh coconut, place it over the kitchen sink and, using a hammer, pierce the soft eye at one end with a nail and drain the liquid into a bowl. If the liquid tastes sweet and fragrant, the coconut is fresh. If it tastes oily and sour, the coconut is rancid and should be thrown away. Crack open the nut with the hammer and remove the oily, white flesh from the shell, peeling off the brown inner skin with a potato peeler. Canned coconut milk is the closest substitute for fresh coconut milk. It is produced by removing the shell, husk and water and then pressing the fresh coconut flesh. Coconut cream is thicker than coconut milk because it contains less water and creamed coconut, sold in blocks, is even more concentrated. These offer a slightly sweeter flavour to Indian dishes. Coconut powder is also available commercially and is a great storecupboard standby for quick Indian curries and desserts.

Mango (aam) – Mangoes are considered the king of fruits in India. They come in hundreds of varieties and different sizes, with colours ranging from green to bright orange and red. The ripe fruit has a peach-like flesh, with a sweet and creamy taste and a perfumed aroma. Mangoes are used in chutneys, pickles, curries, drinks and desserts and are eaten on their own.

Mung bean sprouts (moong) – In Maharashtra, Gujarat and Andhra Pradesh, whole mung beans are sprouted and eaten as a salad (see page 164) or a starter. Sprouting the beans makes them much easier to digest (see page 18).

Okra (bhindi) – Of all the exotic vegetables, Indians love okra the most. Okra is also called gumbo or lady fingers. The green skin is slightly fuzzy and, inside, the flesh has rows of creamy white seeds. Okra must be washed and dried thoroughly before cooking. The pods mustn't be damp when you cut them and you mustn't wash okra after you have cut it, or it will exude a sticky substance. Avoid pods with blemishes and choose a stem that snaps cleanly. The pods should be firm and not mushy.

HERBS, SPICES AND FLAVOURINGS

Ajowan seeds (ajowan) – Native to southern India, this seed is closely related to caraway and cumin, though it tastes strongly of thyme. It has a distinct, pungent aroma and a sharp taste so it is used in moderation. It is known for its carminative properties and is used, therefore, in rich, deep-fried preparations and bean recipes.

Asafoetida (hing) – Powerful and pungent, asafoetida is a dried yellow-brown resin obtained from the roots of the fennel plant. The plants are native to Central Asia, from Iran to Afghanistan. Asafoetida is a spice generally used with vegetables rather than meat. So, although its natural habitat lies in the north, asafoetida is associated with South India, where vegetarianism is most common. Only a tiny amount is used for any dish – the resin is fried in hot oil so that it can be easily dispersed throughout the other ingredients. The high temperature changes the taste, releasing an aroma that is reminiscent of raw onion and garlic. Asafoetida is used in lentil dishes to ease the digestion of pulses and beans, as well as in curries, pickles and chutneys.

Bay leaf (tej patta) – The type of bay leaf used in Indian cooking is the leaf of the cassia tree. These leaves are long, thin and light green in colour, with a mellow, spicy aroma and a sweet taste. In Indian cooking, the bay leaf is used as a flavouring in meat and rice dishes and it is an important component in the Moghul style of cuisine. One or two dried leaves are sufficient to scent a dish and they can be removed easily before serving.

Black cardamom (badi elaichi) – Black cardamom is not true cardamom, but a related variety, the flavour and texture of which are not as delicate as those of the green cardamom. Dried black cardamom pods are actually dark brown in colour, rough and ribbed on the surface. The oval pods are about 2.5cm/1in long. Peeling back the leathery skin releases a woody, smoky, camphoraceous aroma and reveals a mass of about 40 hard, sticky, tar-coloured seeds encased in a soft, sweet-smelling pulp. An invaluable spice in any tandoori-style recipe of northern India, black cardamom is an important component in spice blends such as Garam Masala (see page 23). Unlike green cardamom, it is never used in sweet dishes, but is reserved solely for savoury cooking.

Cassia (dalchini) — Although closely related to cinnamon and often confused with it, cassia bark comes from Burma, while cinnamon's birthplace is Sri Lanka. Like cinnamon, cassia comes from the bark of an evergreen laurel tree. The bark is peeled from thin branches, then dried in the sun to form quills or cassia sticks. The aroma of cassia is highly perfumed, penetrating, sweet and lingering. The flavour has an agreeable bitterness and is more robust than cinnamon. Cassia is used in Garam Masala (see page 23) and for flavouring rice dishes and curries, certain sweets and Indian tea. Cinnamon can be used in place of cassia bark, but many supermarkets now stock cassia.

Chilli (mirchi) — There are hundreds of varieties of chillies in the world, but Indian cooks tend to favour the long, slender, green variety. When buying fresh chillies, make sure the skins are smooth and shiny. The general rule of thumb is the smaller the chilli, the hotter it is. The heat of the chilli depends upon the amount of capsaicin, a volatile oil found in the seeds and the pith of the chilli. The seeds of the chilli can be removed and discarded if desired, but this will give a milder taste to the dish. For the recipes in this book, do not remove any of the seeds. Chilli powder is a substitute for fresh green chillies and often a dish requires both. Many commonly available chilli powders are a blend of a number of spices and seasonings. The heat of these blends varies, so it is worth testing in advance or using a small amount when you cook with them the first time. Large dried red chillies tend to be milder in heat than small ones. They are useful to have in your storecupboard because they last longer than fresh ones. For the most flavour, chillies tend to be dry roasted or heated in oil before using.

Clove (laung) — Cloves are dark brown in colour and have a sharp, pungent taste and fragrant aroma. These dried unopened flower buds are bitter on their own but the heat of the cooking tones down their flavours.

Coriander (dhania) — The plant *Coriandrum sativum* yields both the pungent-smelling spice known as coriander seed and the highly aromatic herb known as coriander leaf. In Indian cooking, the seeds are an important component in the northern spice blend Garam Masala (see page 23), and are generally ground or crushed before use. Fresh coriander leaves are used extensively in Indian cooking and as a garnish. They are best stored in the fridge in an airtight container and should always be rinsed well before use. The best way to clean coriander is to place it in a bowl of cold water and swish it around with your hands to remove any grit or dirt particles.

Cumin seeds (jeera) – Greenish-yellow cumin seeds resemble caraway and are an integral part of Indian cooking. The slightly bitter yet warming flavour makes one think of curry. They have an earthy, warm, pungent aroma and taste pungent, spicy and sweet.

Curry leaf (kari patta) – These small, shiny leaves, about 2.5cm/1in long, are used whole in Indian cooking, much like bay leaves. The leaves, which have a citrus scent, lend a dish a distinct curry aroma. Curry leaves are generally heated in oil to release their flavour. Once heated, they look shrivelled and crispy. Fresh curry leaves can be stored in a sealed plastic bag in the fridge for up to 1 week.

Fennel seeds (saunf) – The greenish-yellow seeds of fennel resemble cumin, but are slightly fatter and larger. They impart a strong anise flavour that is warm and menthol-like. It is one of the important spices in the East Indian spice mixture known as Panch Phoron (see page 24) and is also used to flavour drinks and sweets.

Fenugreek seeds (methi) – Rectangular in shape and brownish-yellow in colour, fenugreek seeds are generally fried or toasted whole before use to reduce their bitterness. Ground fenugreek tastes strong, bitter and intensely aromatic. It is used as a pickling spice and is one of the spices in the East Indian spice mixture Panch Phoron (see page 24).

Ginger (adrak) – Although a root, ginger is used like a spice. It adds a touch of heat to savoury Indian dishes. The skin can be peeled with a knife or scraped off with a metal spoon before the root is grated or chopped. Look for pieces that are not wrinkled. Indians often add ginger at the end of cooking – the flavour is quite strong when eaten almost raw.

Green cardamom (elaichi) – After saffron and vanilla, cardamom is the third most expensive spice in the world. Dried cardamom pods are pale green, oval, knobbly in shape and about 1cm/½in long. When the peppery husk is crushed open, three seed segments, each containing three or four brown-black, oily, pungent seeds are revealed. The taste of the seeds is warm and camphoraceous. Cardamom is used in both sweet and savoury dishes and many spice blends, as well as Indian tea. Black cardamom pods are generally used whole in Indian cooking; however, the seeds of the green cardamom pods are often used on their own without the husks. To remove the seeds of green cardamom pods, place them on a flat surface and, using the back of a spoon, crush them until the casings split open. Green cardamom can also be used whole in spice mixtures, where the husks are ground along with the seeds.

Mango powder (amchur/amchoor) – Made from raw green mangoes that are cut, dried in the sun and pounded into a powder, mango powder is used as a souring agent in Indian cooking, adding a tangy taste to dishes without adding moisture. It is often sprinkled over meat to tenderize it.

Mustard seeds (rai) — Mustard seeds come from three large shrubs, *Brassica juncea* (brown mustard), *B. nigra* (black mustard) and *B. hirta* (white mustard). All three produce bright yellow flowers that die off to leave small round seeds. The brown seeds, which are small, matt and hard, are the ones predominantly used in Indian cooking. When heated they taste bitter, nutty, hot and aromatic.

Nigella seeds (kalonji) — The *Nigella* plant is grown predominantly in India and although the seeds are also known as onion seeds, they have nothing to with onions. The seeds have very little odour but release a scent similar to oregano when rubbed between your fingers. They have a nutty, bitter flavour and are one of the five spices in the East Indian blend known as Panch Phoron (see page 24). They are also added to bread doughs.

Pomegranate seeds (anardana) — These are the sun-dried fruit kernels of the plant *Punica granatum*. Pomegranate seeds are used extensively in the cuisines of the northern and northwestern regions, where they are often ground to impart a piquant flavour to snacks such as samosas and to curries.

Saffron (kesar) — Saffron is the dried stigma of *Crocus sativus*, an autumn-flowering plant. More than 250,000 crocus flowers must be harvested to obtain 450g/1lb of saffron and the stigmas need to be collected by hand, which is why saffron is the single most expensive spice. Almost all religious festival sweets and puddings are laced with saffron. It has a strong, penetrating, clinging aroma and a warm, rich flavour. Steep the stigmas in water or milk for a few minutes before use to extract as much of the flavour as possible.

Tamarind (imli) — The tangy fruit of the tamarind tree grows in large, seeded, pulp-filled pods. Used to add tartness to Indian recipes, the pulp is available in an almost-black cake form resembling a pack of dates or in a liquid concentrate.

Turmeric (haldi) — Turmeric is the incredibly versatile spice that comes from the root of the *Curcuma longa*, a leafy plant belonging to the ginger family. It is mildly aromatic and tastes pungent, bitter and earthy. Although it is often used as a substitute for saffron, the flavour is entirely different. In India, turmeric is used as a mild digestive and remedy for liver ailments and it possesses other medicinal qualities.

NUTS (DAANE)

Nuts are used in Indian cooking to thicken gravies, enrich puddings, garnish dishes and create Indian sweets such as the fudge known as barfi.

Almond (badaam) — The almond is the most important nut in Indian cooking. It is used to make velvety smooth sauces for curries, luscious desserts and as a garnish for Moghul dishes.

Cashew nut (kaaju) — This kidney-shaped nut is found mainly in the cuisine of southern India. It is chopped, lightly fried and added to both sweet and savoury dishes, including curries, desserts and snacks.

Pistachio (pista) — In addition to its use as a roasted, salty snack, the raw, unsalted pistachio is used in Indian cooking, especially in desserts, rice dishes and Indian Milk Fudge (see page 179).

PULSES (DAL)

Pulses can be grouped into three broad categories: lentils, beans and peas. There are hulled, split ones with the skin removed and unhulled varieties with the skin still intact. Lentils do not need soaking and are easier to cook than whole beans. Red and yellow lentils are actually split so they are even quicker to cook. This means that you cannot replace a split lentil with a whole bean in a recipe. It is acceptable to use tinned pulses and beans for the recipes, but make sure you drain and rinse them thoroughly before cooking. If using dried pulses, check through them for stones (this is especially important if you have bought them in bulk from a whole-food or Indian food shop, but less so for those bought from a supermarket), then put them in a sieve and rinse under cold running water before cooking.

Bengal gram (chana dal/Bengal gram dal) — Closely related to the chickpea, *Bengal gram* is smaller, often split and tastes sweeter, which means it can be used to make Indian sweets. Bengal gram can be found in Asian food shops.

Black-eyed beans (chawli/lobhia/rongi) — Indians from the southwest use black-eyed beans in abundance, cooked in stews and braised in dishes with spices. In northern India they are prepared in similar ways to kidney beans.

Dried beans — After lentils, dried beans are the second-most common pulse consumed in India. They need soaking and the longer you store them, the longer you need to cook them because they toughen with age. The green split mung bean (*moong dal*) is light and delicate when cooked, looking cream or yellow in colour with flecks of green.

Lentils (dal) — The two most popular lentils in Indian cuisine, and the ones used in the recipes in this book, are yellow lentils (*tuvar* or *arhar dal*) and red lentils (*masoor dal*). Lentils are the easiest pulses to digest and the quickest to cook. Yellow lentils are sometimes sold with an oily coating that should be rinsed off before cooking.

STORECUPBOARD INGREDIENTS

Basmati rice (basmati chawal) — Basmati, meaning
the queen of fragrance, is a long-grain rice grown in the
foothills of the Himalayas. Once cooked, the grains stay firm
and separate, are spongy to the touch and exude an earthy
and nutty aroma. There are several varieties and grades
of basmati rice, which you might have to purchase and test
before choosing the one that you personally like. Store rice
and other grains in a cool, dry cupboard.

Chickpea or gram flour (besan) — This flour is pale
yellow in colour, silky in texture and has a pleasant, nutty
aroma. It is used in the preparation of both savoury and sweet
Indian dishes. Be careful not to confuse gram flour with
graham flour, which is made from wheat. Like all flours,
gram flour should be stored in a cool, dry place, away from
direct sunlight, as exposure to heat can cause it to go off and
take on a stale, rancid taste.

Oils (tel) — The oils used in Indian cooking vary according
to the regional style of cuisine, which is determined by a
region's climate and geography. Most dishes are cooked in
vegetable oil. In northern India, groundnut oil is traditionally
used for frying; in the east it is mustard oil; and in the south
coconut oil is favoured. The recipes in this book use mostly
vegetable oil and, occasionally, groundnut oil, which you
will find in Asian food shops.

Poppadums (papad) — Poppadums are thin wafers
made from lentils, oil and spices and are served as a cocktail
accompaniment or simply as a snack. To deep-fry them,
immerse them one at a time into vegetable oil heated to
180–200°C/350–400°F for 4–5 seconds until they crinkle and
expand, turning a pale gold colour. Remove the poppadums
immediately from the oil, shake off the excess and drain on
kitchen paper. Alternatively, you can brush both sides of the
poppadum with a little oil and place it under a medium-hot
grill, turning it once when brown spots appear on one side.
Once cooked, poppadums can be served at once, or stored
in an airtight container at room temperature for 5–6 days.

Rice flour (Chawal ka atta) — Rice flour is a fine,
white powder made from grinding white long grain rice.
Free from gluten, it is often used in Indian cooking as an
alternative to wheat flour to make Indian-style flatbreads
such as South Indian appams or soft breads. Rice flour also
acts as a binding and thickening agent. You can make your
own rice flour by pulverizing uncooked Basmati rice grains
in an electric grinder but it is also available in speciality shops
and in most supermarkets.

TECHNIQUES

CHOPPING MANGOES

Use a sharp knife to slice the flesh away from the central stone, to yield two thick pieces. Make criss-cross cuts in the flesh without cutting through the peel, then bend the peel back and carefully cut the flesh away from it. Don't forget to cut away any flesh from around the stone.

DRY ROASTING SPICES (BHUNA)

Dry-roast, or toast, spices by warming them in a hot, dry pan over a medium-low heat until they release their aroma. Watch carefully so they do not burn and tip them out of the pan as soon as you can smell the aroma. This method enhances the flavours of the spices. After they cool, they are usually ground to a powder. This procedure is also used in making various spice mixtures such as Garam Masala (see page 23). The spices are then ready for use in Indian dishes.

FRYING SPICES (TAKDA/BAGHAR)

Heat some oil or melt some ghee or butter in a hot pan and add the spices, which are often whole but sometimes ground. Fry them until they splutter and sizzle. They shouldn't burn. This process, which intensifies the flavours of a dish, is either carried out as the first step in cooking, before adding the onions, for example, or as the last stage when this spice-perfumed oil is then added to a dish as a final touch or a garnish. The garnishing technique is often used for lentil dishes, chutneys, salads and vegetable recipes.

PEELING TOMATOES

With a small, sharp knife, cut a cross in the skin at the base of the tomato. Place it in a heatproof bowl, pour over boiling water to cover and leave for 30 seconds. Use a slotted spoon to remove the tomato, then use the knife to peel away the skin.

REMOVING PRAWNS' VEINS

Cut along the back of the prawn using a small, sharp knife, without cutting all the way through. Lift out the dark digestive tract, using the tip of the knife, then remove any remnants of the vein under cold running water.

SPROUTING MUNG BEANS

Rinse the mung beans, then put them in a bowl, cover with warm water and leave for at least 8 hours or overnight. Drain and rinse the beans, put them in a clean, damp, muslin cloth and tie it to enclose them. Leave in a warm place for another 8 hours, or until the outer casings of the beans begin to crack and tiny white sprouts appear. Sprinkle with a little warm water once or twice while the beans are sprouting in the cloth to prevent them drying out. Rinse the sprouted beans and use immediately, or wrap in a damp cloth and refrigerate until required. However, they need to be cooked within 48 hours.

CHUTNEYS AND SPICE MIXTURES

MANGO CHUTNEY
AAM KI CHUTNEY

SERVES 4
PREPARATION TIME: 10 MINUTES
COOKING TIME: 15 MINUTES

Chutneys in India tend to be sharp and sour and are served with a main meal or as a side relish for savoury snacks. Although there are countless commercial mango chutneys available, it is rare to find one with noticeable thick chunks of fruit throughout.

3 tbsp **vegetable oil**

1 large ripe **mango**, peeled and roughly chopped (*see page 18*)

2.5cm/1in piece **root ginger**, peeled and grated

2 tbsp **sugar**

1 tbsp **malt vinegar**

½ tsp **chilli powder**

½ tsp **salt**

1 **HEAT** the oil in a heavy-based saucepan over a low heat.

2 **ADD** the mango, ginger, sugar, vinegar, chilli powder and salt and cook, stirring occasionally, for 15 minutes, or until the mango is soft.

3 **REMOVE** the pan from the heat and leave the chutney to cool completely.

4 **TRANSFER** the cool chutney to an airtight container and refrigerate for up to 2 weeks.

MINT AND YOGURT CHUTNEY
PUDINA RAITA

SERVES 4
PREPARATION TIME: 10 MINUTES

2 **green chillies**, roughly chopped

a generous handful **mint leaves**

1 bunch **coriander leaves**, roughly chopped

1 **onion**, roughly chopped

4 tbsp **natural yogurt**

1 tbsp **lemon juice**

½ tsp **salt**

1 **PUT** all of the ingredients in a blender and blend until the mixture forms a thick, coarse paste.

2 **TRANSFER** the chutney to an airtight container and refrigerate for up to 4 days.

VARIATION
CORIANDER CHUTNEY – Put 2 bunches roughly chopped coriander leaves, 2 chopped green chillies, 1 teaspoon lemon juice, 1 teaspoon sugar and ½ teaspoon salt in a blender and blend until a fine paste forms. Add 2 tablespoons water if the mixture seems too dry. Transfer to an airtight container and refrigerate for up to 4 days.

COCONUT AND TOMATO CHUTNEY

MYSORE CHUTNEY

SERVES 4
PREPARATION TIME: 10 MINUTES
COOKING TIME: 5 MINUTES

*Fresh coconut marks this flavoursome chutney with a subtle
sweetness that is nicely balanced by the heat of the dried chillies.
If fresh coconut is not available, unsweetened desiccated coconut
makes a suitable substitute.*

2 tbsp **tamarind pulp**

2 tbsp **groundnut oil**

6 **dried red chillies**, stalks removed

2 **tomatoes**, roughly chopped

½ **coconut** (about 200g/7oz), peeled and broken into pieces

½ tsp **salt**

6 **curry leaves**

½ tsp **brown mustard seeds**

½ tsp **cumin seeds**

a pinch **asafoetida**

1 PUT the tamarind pulp in a heatproof bowl, pour over
enough boiling water to cover and leave to stand for
10 minutes. Use a wooden spoon to press the pulp and

release the fibres and seeds, then strain through a nylon
sieve into a bowl, using the back of the spoon to extract as
much juice as possible. Discard the tamarind pulp and set
aside the juice.

2 HEAT 1 tablespoon of the oil in a frying pan over
a medium heat. Add the chillies and fry, stirring constantly,
for 30 seconds, or until they sizzle. Watch the chillies
carefully so they do not burn.

3 TRANSFER the chillies to a blender with the tomatoes,
coconut, salt, tamarind juice and 2 tablespoons water and
blend until a fairly smooth paste forms. Tip the chutney
into a bowl and set aside.

4 HEAT the remaining 1 tablespoon oil in the wiped-out pan
over a medium heat. Add the curry leaves, mustard seeds,
cumin seeds and asafoetida and fry, stirring constantly,
for 30 seconds, or until the seeds begin to splutter.
Watch carefully so they do not burn.

5 SPOON this mixture over the coconut and tomato
chutney and stir well. The chutney is now ready to serve,
or it can be left to cool, transferred to an airtight container
and refrigerated for 3–4 days. Remove it from the fridge
about 10 minutes before serving so the flavour of the
coconut isn't masked by the cold.

TOMATO CHUTNEY

TAMATAR CHUTNEY

SERVES 4
PREPARATION TIME: 10 MINUTES, PLUS COOLING TIME
COOKING TIME: 12 MINUTES

Tomato and tamarind combine to create a tangy, aromatic chutney. This recipe works just as well with canned tomatoes, if fresh ones are not in season.

2 tbsp **tamarind pulp**

450g/1lb **tomatoes**, peeled (*see page 18*) and chopped

2 **garlic** cloves, chopped

1 tsp **sugar**

1 tsp **chilli powder**

1 tsp **salt**

¼ tsp **turmeric**

1 tbsp **groundnut oil**

6 **curry leaves**

¼ tsp **brown mustard seeds**

a pinch **asafoetida**

1 PUT the tamarind pulp in a heatproof bowl, pour over enough boiling water to cover and leave to stand for 10 minutes. Use a wooden spoon to press the pulp and release the fibres and seeds, then strain through a nylon sieve into a bowl, using the back of the spoon to extract as much juice as possible. Discard the tamarind pulp and set aside the juice.

2 PUT the tomatoes in a large saucepan over a medium heat. Add the garlic, sugar, chilli powder, salt, turmeric and tamarind juice and bring to the boil, stirring. Reduce the heat to low and leave the mixture to simmer for 10 minutes, stirring occasionally, to blend the flavours and thicken. Remove the pan from the heat and set aside until the chutney cools completely.

3 TRANSFER the chutney to a blender and blend until a smooth paste forms. Spoon the chutney into a glass jar with a tight-fitting, non-metallic lid, but do not close.

4 HEAT the oil in a frying pan over a medium heat. Add the curry leaves, mustard seeds and asafoetida and fry, stirring constantly, for 30 seconds, or until the seeds splutter. Watch carefully so they do not burn.

5 TIP the spice mixture into the chutney and mix well. The chutney is now ready to use, or it can be left to cool in the glass jar, then sealed and refrigerated for up to 2 weeks.

CUCUMBER RELISH
KHEERA RAITA

SERVES 4
PREPARATION TIME: 5 MINUTES, PLUS CHILLING

A raita is a yogurt-based condiment usually containing vegetables. Raitas are designed to be cooling, to counteract the effects of any spicy hot dishes. So, if you find a curry too fiery, balance the heat with a milk-based preparation such as this one.

½ **cucumber**, coarsely grated

300ml/10½fl oz/1¼ cups **natural yogurt**, whisked

¼ tsp **salt**

¼ tsp **ground cumin**

a pinch freshly ground **black pepper**

a pinch **chilli powder**

1 SQUEEZE any excess water from the grated cucumber, using your hands.

2 PLACE the cucumber in a bowl, then stir in the yogurt.

3 STIR in the salt, cumin, black pepper and chilli powder. Cover the bowl with cling film and refrigerate until required. Serve chilled.

VARIATION
ONION AND YOGURT RELISH – Put 300ml/10½fl oz/ 1¼ cups natural yogurt in a large bowl and whisk until smooth. Stir in 1 chopped onion, 1 finely chopped green chilli and ¼ teaspoon salt. Heat 1 tablespoon vegetable oil in a frying pan over a medium heat, add 6 curry leaves and ¼ teaspoon brown mustard seeds and fry, stirring constantly, until the spices splutter. Watch carefully so they do not burn. Immediately tip the mixture into the yogurt and stir well. Cover the bowl with cling film and refrigerate until required. Serve chilled.

GARLIC, YOGURT AND PEANUT RELISH – Put 300ml/ 10½fl oz/1¼ cups natural yogurt in a large bowl and whisk until smooth. Stir in 2 peeled and crushed garlic cloves, 1 finely chopped green chilli, ¼ tsp salt and a handful of finely chopped coriander leaves. Heat 1 tablespoon of vegetable oil in a frying pan over a medium heat and add 10-15 skinned and unsalted crushed peanuts. Fry for 1 minute, or until the peanuts turn golden brown. Turn off the heat and leave to cool. Stir the peanuts into the yogurt relish, cover the bowl with cling film and refrigerate until required. Serve chilled.

LEMON PICKLE
NIMBU KA ACHAAR

SERVES 4
PREPARATION TIME: 10 MINUTES, PLUS 30 MINUTES SOAKING TIME
AND 1 WEEK'S MATURING TIME

Most Indian pickles are prepared with various spices and oil, rather than vinegar. The oil in this recipe comes from the skin of the lemons.

12 **lemons**
150g/5½oz **salt**
300g/10½oz/1⅓ cups **sugar**
1 tbsp **ajowan seeds**
6 **dried red chillies**

1 WASH the lemons, then leave them to soak in cold water to cover for 30 minutes. Dry the lemons, then top and tail them and cut each into 8 pieces.
2 PLACE the lemons and the remaining ingredients in a non-metallic bowl and mix together.
3 TRANSFER the pickle mixture to a large glass jar with a non-metallic lid, seal and leave in a warm place for 1 week, before using.
4 SHAKE the jar gently at least once a day to ensure the liquid released from the lemons covers the lemons. When the lemons begin to turn dark, the pickle is ready to eat. Refrigerate after opening. The pickle will keep for up to 3 months in the fridge.

GARAM MASALA
GARAM MASALA

MAKES ABOUT 5 TBSP
PREPARATION TIME: 5 MINUTES
COOKING TIME: 2 MINUTES

Garam masala quite literally means a mixture of hot spices and is a blend of dry-roasted whole spices from northern India that are ground to a powder. Garam masala is usually added at the end of cooking to finish off a dish with a delicate aroma of roasted spices, but it can also be added with other spices during cooking. Once you've made this, you'll find there is no comparison between a fresh blend you make at home and the shop-bought varieties that have been sitting on a shelf for months.

4 pieces **cinnamon stick** or **cassia bark**, each 5cm/2in long
12 **bay leaves**
5 **black cardamom pods**
20 **green cardamom pods**
2 tbsp **coriander seeds**
2 tbsp **cumin seeds**
1 tsp **cloves**
1 tsp **black peppercorns**

1 HEAT a dry frying pan over a medium-low heat until you can feel the heat rising. Add the cinnamon stick or cassia bark, bay leaves and black cardamom and roast for 30 seconds, shaking the pan.
2 ADD the remaining spices and continue roasting, shaking the pan, for about a further 1 minute, or until you can

smell the aroma of the spices. Watch carefully so they
do not burn.

3 REMOVE the pan from the heat and immediately tip
the spices on to a plate and leave to cool completely.

4 TRANSFER the spices to a spice mill and blend until
finely ground. Store the mixture in an airtight container,
away from direct sunlight, for up to 6 months.

VARIATIONS

PANCH PHORON – Heat a dry frying pan over a medium-
low heat. Add 4 dried red chillies, ½ teaspoon *each* brown
mustard seeds, fenugreek seeds, nigella seeds and fennel
seeds and roast, shaking the pan constantly, for about
3 minutes, or until you can smell the aroma. Watch carefully
so the seeds do not burn. Leave to cool completely, then
grind and store as above.

DHANSAK MASALA – Heat a dry frying pan over a
medium-low heat. Add a 5cm/2in piece cinnamon stick or
cassia bark, 20 green cardamom pods, 2 teaspoons *each* cumin
and coriander seeds, 1 teaspoon *each* black peppercorns,
brown mustard seeds and fenugreek seeds, 4 bay leaves and
½ teaspoon *each* cloves and turmeric. Roast, shaking the pan
constantly, for about 3 minutes, or until you can smell the
aroma of the spices. Watch carefully so they do not burn.
Leave to cool completely, then grind and store as above.

MANJU'S QUICK CURRY PASTE
MANJU KI JHATPAT MASALA

MAKES 6½ TBSP
PREPARATION TIME: 5 MINUTES

*This blend of spices and other ingredients is used to create a flavourful
curry sauce. This paste provides a base to a medium-hot, tangy curry.*

2 tbsp **vegetable oil**
2 tsp **tomato purée**
2 tsp **ground cumin**
2 tsp **ground coriander**
1 tsp **turmeric**
½ tsp **Garam Masala** (*see page 23*)
¼ tsp **chilli powder**
¼ tsp **salt**

1 MIX all the ingredients in a small bowl to form a thick,
reddish-brown paste.

2 USE at once, or transfer to an airtight container and
refrigerate for up to 9 days.

MADRAS CURRY PASTE
GEELA MASALA

MAKES 7–8 TBSP
PREPARATION TIME: 10 MINUTES, PLUS COOLING TIME
COOKING TIME: 7 MINUTES

The pungent coriander and cumin, spicy black pepper and nutty brown mustard featured in this curry paste create an authentic taste of southern India.

1 tbsp **black peppercorns**

4 tbsp **coriander seeds**

2 tbsp **cumin seeds**

1 tsp **brown mustard seeds**

125ml/4fl oz/½ cup **vegetable oil**

6 **garlic** cloves, crushed

5cm/2in piece **root ginger**, peeled and chopped

1 tbsp **chilli powder**

1 tbsp **turmeric**

1 HEAT a dry frying pan over a medium-low heat. Add the peppercorns and the coriander, cumin and mustard seeds and roast, shaking the pan occasionally, until you can smell the aroma. Watch the spices carefully so they do not burn. Remove the pan from the heat and immediately tip the spices on to a plate and leave to cool completely.

2 TRANSFER the spices to a spice mill and blend until finely ground, then set aside.

3 POUR the oil into a saucepan over a medium heat. Add the garlic, ginger, chilli powder and turmeric and stir well. Tip in the freshly ground spices and fry, stirring constantly, for 30 seconds to 1 minute until the oil separates.

4 REMOVE the pan from the heat and leave the paste to cool completely. Transfer the paste to an airtight container and store, away from direct sunlight, for up to 6 months.

VARIATION

GREEN MASALA PASTE – Heat a dry frying pan over a medium-low heat, add a 5cm/2in piece cinnamon stick or cassia bark, 9 black peppercorns, 4 cloves and 1 teaspoon cumin seeds and roast until you can smell the aroma. Watch the spices carefully so they do not burn. Immediately tip the spices on to a plate and leave to cool completely, then put them in a spice mill and blend until finely ground. Tip into a blender and add a 5cm/2in piece peeled and chopped root ginger, 5 chopped garlic cloves, 2 chopped green chillies, 1 chopped onion, a handful coriander leaves, 9 mint leaves, 2 tablespoons vegetable oil, 1 tablespoon lemon juice and ¼ teaspoon salt and blend until a coarse, light green paste forms. Store as above.

BREADS

NAANS
NAANS

MAKES 4
PREPARATION TIME: 15 MINUTES, PLUS AT LEAST 30 MINUTES
RISING TIME COOKING TIME: 10–15 MINUTES

Naan, the Persian word for bread, refers in Indian cookery to this oval flatbread made with white wheat flour and usually leavened with yeast. Milk or yogurt is added for greater volume. Naans are traditionally made in a tandoor – a large, charcoal-heated, bowl-shaped oven. The breads are placed on the inside walls of the oven and baked in minutes. Although tandoor-baked naans are more rustic looking and larger than those made in a domestic oven, yours will taste the same. Naans can be cooked the day before, stored in an airtight container and reheated in an oven at 180°C/350°F/Gas 4 for 5 minutes. To prevent them drying out, sprinkle them with a few drops of water and wrap them in foil before reheating.

1 tsp **dried yeast**

1 tsp **sugar**

200g/7oz/1⅔ cups **plain flour**, plus extra for dusting

½ tsp **baking powder**

¼ tsp **salt**

1 tbsp **vegetable oil**, plus extra for greasing the baking tray

2 tbsp **natural yogurt**

2 tbsp **milk**

1 PUT the yeast in a small bowl and stir in 1 tablespoon warm water. Stir in the sugar and leave in a warm place, uncovered, for 5 minutes, or until bubbles appear and the mixture looks a little frothy.

2 COMBINE the flour, baking powder and salt in a large bowl. Make a well in the centre. Pour the oil, yogurt and milk into the well, then add the yeast mixture. Mix until a soft dough forms. If the dough is dry and doesn't come together, sprinkle over 1–2 tablespoons water.

3 KNEAD the dough by clenching your hand into a fist, then wet your knuckles and press them repeatedly into the dough, pressing against the side of the bowl, until a soft, smooth dough forms. This should take about 10 minutes.

4 COVER the bowl with a clean, damp tea towel or cling film and leave the dough in a warm place to rise until it increases in volume and is no longer sticky. This will take at least 30 minutes, but ideally leave for 3–4 hours.

5 PREHEAT the oven to 200°C/400°F/Gas 6 and lightly grease a baking tray large enough to hold 4 naans.

6 PUNCH down the dough, then divide it into 4 balls of equal size. Lightly flour the work surface and roll each ball into a long oval shape about 5mm/¼in thick. Do not roll them too thin, or they will be too crispy.

7 PUT the naans on the baking tray, place them in the centre of the oven and bake for 10–12 minutes until they puff up slightly and are golden and flaky. Serve hot.

EXOTIC LEAVENED NAANS

PESHWARI NAANS

MAKES 4   PREPARATION TIME: 15 MINUTES, PLUS AT LEAST
30 MINUTES RISING TIME   COOKING TIME: 10–15 MINUTES

The Peshwari naan is a popular variation on the traditional plain naan (see page 26). These breads, thought to have come from Peshawar, in Pakistan, are filled with a mixture of nuts and dried fruits. This recipe includes desiccated coconut, a popular ingredient in the Peshwari naans in Western restaurants, although not commonly used in Pakistan. Most traditional recipes use yeast, but self-raising flour is used here for more convenience.

vegetable oil for greasing the baking tray

200g/7oz/1⅔ cups **self-raising flour**, plus extra for dusting

4 tbsp **single cream**

2 tbsp **natural yogurt**

1 tbsp **ground almonds**

1 tbsp **desiccated coconut**

1 tbsp **caster sugar**

1 tbsp **sultanas**

1 PREHEAT the oven to 200°C/400°F/Gas 6 and lightly grease a baking tray large enough to hold 4 naans.

2 PLACE the flour in a large mixing bowl and make a well in the centre. Pour the cream, yogurt and 3 tablespoons water into the well and mix until a soft dough forms. If the dough is dry and doesn't come together, sprinkle over 1–2 tablespoons water.

3 KNEAD the dough by clenching your hand into a fist, then wet your knuckles and press them repeatedly into the dough, pressing against the side of the bowl, until a soft, pliable dough forms. This should take about 10 minutes.

4 COVER the bowl with a clean, damp tea towel or cling film and leave in a warm place to rise until the dough increases in volume and is no longer sticky. This will take at least 30 minutes.

5 DIVIDE the dough into 4 equal-sized balls. Lightly dust the work surface with flour and roll each ball into a long oval shape about 5mm/¼in thick. Do not roll them too thin, or they will be too crispy.

6 COMBINE the ground almonds, desiccated coconut, sugar and sultanas in a bowl. Sprinkle this mixture along the centre of each piece of dough, then fold the dough over to enclose the filling. Press the edges together to seal. Re-roll each piece into a long oval shape.

7 PUT the naans on the greased baking tray, place them on the middle shelf of the oven and bake for 10–12 minutes until they puff up slightly and are golden and flaky. Serve hot.

FENUGREEK FLATBREADS

GUJARATI THEPLAS

MAKES 6
PREPARATION TIME: 8 MINUTES, PLUS 15–30 MINUTES RESTING TIME
COOKING TIME: 12 MINUTES

These unleavened flatbreads from Gujarat, in western India, are similar to chapatis. The dough is prepared with wholewheat flour and chickpea or gram flour, which adds nuttiness and extra flavour.

140g/5oz/1 cup **wholewheat flour**, plus extra for dusting

35g/1¼oz/⅓ cup **chickpea** or **gram flour**

a pinch **asafoetida**

a handful **fenugreek leaves**, chopped, or 2 tbsp **dried fenugreek leaves**

½ tsp **turmeric**

½ tsp **cumin seeds**

¼ tsp **chilli powder**

¼ tsp **ground coriander**

¼ tsp **salt**

3 tbsp **vegetable oil**

1 PUT the wholewheat and chickpea or gram flours, asafoetida, fenugreek leaves, turmeric, cumin seeds, chilli powder, coriander and salt in a large bowl and mix well.

2 MAKE a well in the centre. Add 1 tablespoon of the oil to the well, then gradually add 125ml/4fl oz/½ cup warm water and stir until the mixture forms a soft dough. If the dough is dry and doesn't come together, sprinkle over 1–2 tablespoons water.

3 KNEAD the dough by clenching your hand into a fist, then wet your knuckles and press them repeatedly into the dough, pressing against the side of the bowl, until a soft, smooth dough forms. This should take 5–6 minutes.

4 COVER the bowl with a clean, damp tea towel or cling film and leave in a warm place to rest for 15–30 minutes.

5 DIVIDE the dough into 6 balls of equal size, then dust each ball with flour and roll it into a 15cm/6in circle. Dusting each flatbread with a little flour as you roll it out prevents it sticking and allows the rolling pin to move freely.

6 HEAT a shallow frying pan over a medium heat until a splash of water sizzles on the surface. Brush the surface with 1 teaspoon of the oil. Place a flatbread in the pan and cook for 30 seconds to 1 minute, pressing down firmly all over the surface with the back of a tablespoon.

7 FLIP the flatbread over, using tongs, and continue cooking for 1 minute, carefully pressing down firmly so the dough cooks all the way through and brown spots appear.

8 REMOVE the flatbread from the pan. Wrap it in a clean tea towel and then continue cooking the remaining flatbreads in the same way, brushing the surface of the pan with 1 teaspoon oil before placing each flatbread in the pan. Serve warm.

CHAPATIS

CHAPATIS

MAKES 6
PREPARATION TIME: 10 MINUTES
COOKING TIME: 6–8 MINUTES

Chapatis, *made fresh every day, are a type of unleavened bread from northern India. The wholewheat dough is rolled into flat circles and then cooked on a hot, flat griddle called a* tava. *In an Indian meal, chapatis are used as a scoop to pick up vegetable and lentil dishes.*

250g/9oz/1⅔ cups **wholewheat flour**, plus extra for dusting
1 tsp **vegetable oil**
butter or **ghee**, melted, to serve (optional)

1 SIFT the flour into a large bowl, tipping in the bran left in the sieve. Make a well in the centre. Add the oil to the well, then gradually add 150ml/5½fl oz/⅔ cup warm water. Stir until the mixture forms a soft dough. If the dough is dry and does not come together, add 1–2 tablespoons water.

2 KNEAD the dough by clenching your hand into a fist, then wet your knuckles and press them repeatedly into the dough, pressing against the side of the bowl, until a soft, smooth dough forms. This should take about 10 minutes.

3 DIVIDE the dough into 6 balls of equal size. Dust each chapati with a little flour to prevent it sticking and so the rolling pin can move freely, then roll them out on a lightly floured surface into 15cm/6in circles.

4 HEAT a shallow frying pan over a medium heat until a splash of water sizzles on the surface.

5 PLACE a chapati in the pan and cook for 20 seconds, or until the top surface starts to brown slightly.

6 TURN the chapati over, using tongs, and continue cooking for about 30 seconds until the surface is bubbly.

7 FLIP the chapati over again and, using the back of a tablespoon, press firmly around the edge so it puffs up.

8 REMOVE the chapati from the pan and put it on a clean tea towel. Brush with the melted butter or ghee, if using, then wrap it in the towel to keep warm while you cook the remaining chapatis one at a time. Serve warm.

VARIATION

ONION AND CHILLI CHAPATIS – Prepare the Chapatis recipe through step 3, then add 1 small, finely chopped onion, 2 finely chopped green chillies and 1 teaspoon ajowan seeds to the dough. Knead for a further 2 minutes, or until the ingredients are well combined. Follow the Chapatis recipe from step 4 to complete.

POORIS
POORIS

MAKES **8**
PREPARATION TIME: **10** MINUTES
COOKING TIME: **8** MINUTES

These deep-fried unleavened breads are served in Indian fast-food restaurants and are made at home during auspicious celebrations. They are served with either sweet or savoury dishes, such as the tangy Prawn Pooris (see page 60). In eastern India, pooris are also prepared at breakfast.

300g/10¹⁄₂oz/1¹⁄₂ cups **plain flour**

15g/¹⁄₂oz **butter**, softened

vegetable oil for deep-frying, plus extra
for greasing the work surface

1 SIFT the flour into a large bowl, then add the butter and 4 tablespoons warm water. Mix until a soft dough forms.

2 KNEAD the dough by clenching your hand into a fist, then wet your knuckles and press them repeatedly into the dough, pressing against the side of the bowl, until a soft, pliable dough forms. This should take about 10 minutes.

3 DIVIDE the dough into 8 pieces of equal size and cover with a clean, damp tea towel. Lightly grease the work surface. Heat the oil in a deep saucepan or deep-fat fryer until it reaches 190°C/375°F, or until a small piece of the dough puffs up and rises to the surface instantly.

4 ROLL out one piece of dough into a circle 12.5–15cm/5–6in across and about 3mm/¹⁄₈in thick.

5 PLACE the rolled out dough in the hot oil and fry for 30 seconds, or until it puffs up. Use a slotted spoon to turn the poori over; continue frying until it turns light brown.

6 REMOVE the poori from the oil with the slotted spoon, then drain well on kitchen paper, taking care not to squash out too much of the air. Roll out another dough circle and repeat the process until you have rolled out and fried all the poori dough. These pooris can be made in advance and reheated in an oven at 180°C/350°F/Gas 4 for 5 minutes before serving. Serve hot.

VARIATION
SAMOSA PASTRY — The pastry used to make meat- and vegetable-filled samosas is the same as poori dough, except you substitute 2 teaspoons vegetable oil for the butter. Follow the recipe above through step 3, then roll out, shape and fill the dough as explained in the Vegetable Samosa recipe on page 36.

RICE

PLAIN BASMATI RICE
BASMATI CHAWAL

SERVES 4
PREPARATION TIME: 10 MINUTES, PLUS 5 MINUTES STANDING TIME
COOKING TIME: 10–12 MINUTES

The mild taste of plain basmati rice harmonizes well with the aromatic, spicy and often rich flavours of Indian cuisine. The absorption method of cooking rice, used here, is more streamlined than boiling the rice in a copious amount of water and then draining it. With the absorption method, all the water should be absorbed by the time the rice is tender. After cooking, the grains stay firm and separate and are not sticky.

Rice bought from a specialist Asian shop can be soaked for 20–30 minutes before cooking. This allows the grains to absorb water so the heat penetrates more easily and the rice cooks evenly. However, rice bought from a supermarket should be prepared according to the instructions on the packet. Rice can be cooked up to 48 hours in advance but should only be reheated once. It can be reheated over a very low heat in the same pan, covered, with 4 tablespoons water. Or, cover it with foil and place it in a preheated oven at 180°C/350°F/Gas 4 for 10 minutes.

400g/14oz/2 cups **basmati rice**

½ teaspoon **vegetable oil**

a pinch **salt**

1 BRING 750ml/26fl oz/3 cups water to the boil. Put the rice in a sieve and rinse it under cold running water until the water runs clear. This will remove any excess starch.

2 PUT the rice in a saucepan, cover with a tight-fitting lid and place over a high heat.

3 STIR in the oil, salt and boiling water; return to the boil.

4 COVER the pan, reduce the heat to low and leave the rice to simmer for 10–12 minutes. Do not uncover the pan before the rice has cooked for at least 10 minutes. The rice will be tender when all the water is absorbed, holes appear on the surface and some of the grains appear to be pointing up. Test a few grains to make sure the rice is tender. If, at the end of cooking, it is cooked but some of the water remains, drain the rice in a sieve. If the rice is not cooked and all the water has been absorbed, add 4 tablespoons boiling water, cover the pan with the lid and cook for a further 5 minutes.

5 FLUFF the rice with a fork, then cover the pan again and leave to stand for 5 minutes. Serve piping hot.

VARIATION
SWEET RICE

Follow the Plain Basmati Rice recipe through step 4. Put 2 tablespoons milk and 10 saffron strands in a small bowl and leave to infuse for 3–4 minutes. Melt 75g/2¾oz butter or ghee over a medium-high heat in a large saucepan. Add 4 cloves, 4 whole green cardamom pods, 10 coarsely chopped almonds, 10 coarsely chopped pistachio nuts and, if you like, 1 tablespoon sultanas. Stir for 1 minute, then tip in the cooked rice and continue to stir for 2 minutes. Stir in 3 tablespoons sugar, followed by the saffron milk and stir for another minute. Serve hot or cold as a snack or a dessert.

SPICED RICE
PULAO

SERVES **4**
PREPARATION TIME: **7 MINUTES**
COOKING TIME: ABOUT **15 MINUTES**

Pulaos are preparations where every grain of the cooked rice remains separate. This recipe and the variations below are associated with the cookery of the Moghuls – Persian Muslim princes who ruled India for almost 200 years from the 16th century.

2 tbsp **milk**

20 **saffron strands**

400g/14oz/2 cups **basmati rice**

30g/1oz **butter** or **ghee**

5cm/2in piece **cinnamon stick** or **cassia bark**

6 **black peppercorns**

4 **cloves**

4 **green cardamom pods**

2 **black cardamom pods**

2 **bay leaves**

¼ tsp **cumin seeds**

¼ tsp **salt**

1 **PUT** the milk and saffron strands in a small bowl and leave to infuse for 3–4 minutes. Bring 500ml/17fl oz/2 cups water to the boil.

2 **PUT** the rice in a sieve and rinse it under cold running water until the water runs clear. This will remove any excess starch.

3 **MELT** the butter or ghee in a saucepan with a tight-fitting lid over a low heat. Add the cinnamon stick or cassia bark, peppercorns, cloves, green and black cardamom pods, bay leaves, cumin seeds and salt and stir for 30 seconds, or until you can smell the aroma of the spices. Watch carefully so the spices do not burn.

4 **ADD** the rice to the pan and fry, stirring, for 30 seconds.

5 **POUR** the boiling water into the pan, stir once and return to the boil. Cover the pan, reduce the heat to low and leave the rice to simmer for 3 minutes.

6 **STIR** the saffron-flavoured milk into the rice.

7 **PLACE** the lid on the pan and leave the rice to simmer for 7–9 minutes. Do not uncover the pan before the rice has cooked for at least 7 minutes. The rice will be tender when all the liquid is absorbed, holes appear on the surface and some of the grains appear to be pointing up. Test a few grains to make sure the rice is tender.

8 **FLUFF** the rice with a fork, then re-cover the pan and leave to stand for 5 minutes. Serve piping hot.

VARIATIONS

PULAO RICE WITH PEAS – Omit the saffron-flavoured milk. Replace the butter or ghee with 2 tablespoons vegetable oil and heat over a medium heat. Add a 5cm/2in piece cinnamon stick and 4 green cardamom pods and fry, stirring, for 30 seconds, or until you can smell the aroma. Watch so the spices do not burn. Stir in 150g/5½oz/1 cup shelled peas, 1 chopped green chilli and ¼ teaspoon salt, then follow the Spiced Rice recipe from step 4, using 400g/14oz/2 cups basmati rice. Once you reduce the heat and cover the pan, do not uncover for at least 10 minutes.

SAFFRON RICE – Put 2 tablespoons milk and 20 saffron strands in a small bowl and leave to infuse for 3–4 minutes. Melt the butter or ghee over a medium-high heat. Add 4 cloves, 4 green cardamom pods and ¼ teaspoon *each* cumin seeds and salt. Fry, stirring constantly, for 30 seconds, or until you can smell the aroma. Watch so the spices do not burn. Add 1 sliced onion and continue frying for 3 minutes, or until the onion is soft, then follow the Spiced Rice recipe from step 4, using 400g/14oz/2 cups basmati rice and adding the saffron-flavoured milk to the pan after the rice.

TAMARIND RICE – Put the tamarind pulp in a heatproof bowl, pour over enough boiling water to cover and leave to stand for 10 minutes. Use a wooden spoon to press the pulp and release the fibres and seeds, then strain through a nylon sieve into a bowl, using the back of the spoon to extract as much juice as possible. Discard the tamarind pulp and set aside the juice. Omit the saffron-flavoured milk from the Spiced Rice recipe. Replace the butter or ghee with 2 tablespoons groundnut oil and heat over a medium

heat. Add ½ teaspoon brown mustard seeds, 2 dried red chillies, 1 teaspoon hulled split black lentils, a pinch of asafoetida, 6 curry leaves and ¼ teaspoon salt. Fry, stirring constantly, for 30 seconds, or until you can smell the aroma. Watch so the spices do not burn. Stir in the tamarind juice, then follow the Spiced Rice recipe from step 4, using 400g/14oz/2 cups basmati rice. Once you reduce the heat and cover the pan, do not uncover for at least 10 minutes.

TURMERIC RICE – Omit the saffron-flavoured milk. Replace the butter or ghee with 2 tablespoons vegetable oil and heat over a medium heat. Add 1 teaspoon turmeric, ½ teaspoon *each* brown mustard seeds and cumin seeds and ¼ teaspoon salt. Fry, stirring constantly, for 30 seconds, or until you can smell the aroma. Watch so the spices do not burn. Follow the Spiced Rice recipe from step 4, using 400g/14oz/2 cups basmati rice. Once you reduce the heat and cover the pan, do not uncover for at least 10 minutes.

PART 2

THE RECIPES

Variety is the spice of life and a stroll through any Indian **market** proves how completely Indian **cooks** have taken this notion to heart. Cascading piles of delicate fresh coriander, **sun-ripened** fruits and vegetables, and nuts and seeds of every shape, **texture** and colour abound. The air is a riot of **aromas**, some sweet, some spicy, others pungent or earthy. Sacks of **golden** turmeric and fiery chilli powders look like artists' colour pigments, but Indian cooks **transform** them into another art form altogether – one that is surprisingly **accessible** and, as the recipes in this section show, **easy** to recreate in your own home.

Food occupies a central place in Indian life and meals are **social events** that bring family and friends **together**, whether for religious festivals, special occasions or simply supper at the end of an ordinary day. From **cooling** yogurt relishes and **silky** dals to the sharp heat of chilli-infused curries and the subtle **sweetness** of simple nut- and milk-based desserts, these mouthwatering recipes will show you how to bring the **flavours** of India to life, to produce the best Indian meal you've ever **tasted** – and all made by you.

VEGETABLE SAMOSAS *SAMOSAS*

MAKES **16**   PREPARATION TIME: **20** MINUTES   COOKING TIME: **20** MINUTES

2 tbsp **vegetable oil**, plus extra for deep-frying

½ tsp **cumin seeds**

2 **green chillies**, finely chopped

1 **onion**, chopped

¼ tsp **salt**

¼ tsp **ground coriander**

a pinch **Garam Masala** (*see page 23*)

300g/10½oz **potatoes**, peeled, boiled and roughly mashed

a handful **coriander leaves**, chopped

1 recipe quantity **Samosa Pastry** (*see page 30*)

4 tbsp **plain flour** mixed with a little water to make a "glue"

1 **HEAT** the oil in a saucepan over a medium heat. Add the cumin seeds and fry, stirring, for about 30 seconds, or until they splutter. Watch carefully so they do not burn. Add the chillies and onion and continue frying, stirring occasionally, for 6–8 minutes until the onions are golden brown. Add the salt, ground coriander and garam masala and continue stirring for 1 minute. Stir in the mashed potato and coriander leaves.

2 **DIVIDE** the pastry into 8 balls of equal size and roll out on a lightly floured surface into thin 12.5cm/5in rounds, then cut each in half.

3 **APPLY** the "glue" to the straight edge of each semi-circle, then fold the pastry into a cone shape, sealing the pasted straight edge. Hold the cone with the tapered end down and fill it with about 1 tablespoon of the potato mixture.

4 **SEAL** the samosa with a little more "glue", pressing the edges firmly together. Repeat until all the pastry and filling are used.

5 **HEAT** enough oil for deep-frying in a heavy-based saucepan over a high heat or in a deep-fat fryer to 190°C/375°F, or until a small piece of pastry sizzles in the oil and comes to the surface.

6 **FRY** a few samosas at a time for 3–4 minutes until golden brown. Remove with a slotted spoon and drain on kitchen paper. Continue frying the samosas in batches. Return the oil to the correct temperature before adding each new batch. Once fried, these keep in the fridge for up to 2 days. Reheat in an oven at 180°C/350°F/Gas 4 for 10–15 minutes before serving. Refrigerate uncooked samosas for up to 4 days, or freeze for 1 month. Serve hot with Coriander Chutney (see page 19).

ONION FRITTERS *PYAAZ PAKORAS*

MAKES **24**   PREPARATION TIME: **10** MINUTES
COOKING TIME: **15** MINUTES

Pakoras, *sometimes called* bhajis *or* bhajias, *are batter-fried snacks usually eaten as a starter. The batter, made of spiced chickpea or gram flour, is used to coat vegetables or fish to create a variety of fritters.*

200g/7oz/scant 2 cups **chickpea** or **gram flour**

3 **onions**, sliced

1 tsp **cumin seeds**, crushed

1 tsp **coriander seeds**, crushed

¼ tsp **chilli powder**

½ tsp **salt**

vegetable oil for deep-frying

1 SIFT the flour into a large bowl. Add the onions, cumin seeds, coriander seeds, chilli powder and salt. Stir together, then make a well in the centre. Add 4 tablespoons water to the well, then mix with a fork until the mixture forms a thick, stiff batter. If it appears runny, add extra flour.

2 HEAT enough oil for deep-frying in a heavy-based saucepan over a high heat or in a deep-fat fryer to 190°C/375°F, or until a small drop of the batter sizzles fiercely in the oil.

3 DROP 1 tablespoon of the batter into the oil and fry for about 1 minute, or until it turns golden brown.

4 REMOVE the fritter from the oil with a slotted spoon and drain on kitchen paper. Taste the fritter and adjust the seasoning of the batter, adding more salt or chilli powder, if necessary.

5 FRY the remaining fritters, working in batches to avoid overcrowding the pan, if necessary. Remove any pieces of fried batter from the oil and return the oil to the correct temperature before adding each new batch. These fritters can be fried in advance and reheated in an oven at 180°C/350°F/Gas 4 for 10 minutes before serving. Serve hot with Tomato Chutney (see page 21).

POTATO AND CORIANDER FRITTERS

ALOO BHAJIS

**MAKES 16   PREPARATION TIME: 10 MINUTES
COOKING TIME: 15 MINUTES**

The subtle heat of the green chillies, the nuttiness of the gram flour and the cool, refreshing taste of coriander make these fritters a delightful opening to a meal.

250g/9oz **floury potatoes**, peeled

55g/2oz/½ cup **chickpea** or **gram flour**

2 **green chillies**, finely chopped

½ tsp **salt**

a handful **coriander leaves**, finely chopped

vegetable oil for deep-frying

1 GRATE the potatoes coarsely into a large bowl.

2 SIFT the flour into the same bowl, then add the chillies, salt and coriander leaves. Stir together with a fork until the mixture forms a thick, coarse batter.

3 HEAT enough oil for deep-frying in a heavy-based saucepan over a high heat or in a deep-fat fryer to 190ºC/375ºF, or until a small drop of the batter sizzles fiercely in the oil.

4 DROP 1 tablespoon of the batter into the oil and fry for about 1 minute, or until it turns golden brown.

5 REMOVE the fritter from the oil with a slotted spoon and drain on kitchen paper. Taste the fritter and adjust the seasoning of the batter, adding more salt, if necessary.

6 FRY the remaining fritters, working in batches to avoid overcrowding the pan, if necessary. Remove any pieces of fried batter from the oil and return the oil to the correct temperature before adding each new batch. These fritters can be fried in advance and reheated in an oven at 180ºC/350ºF/Gas 4 for 10 minutes before serving. Serve hot with Tomato Chutney (see page 21).

CUMIN AND CORIANDER POTATO PATTIES

ALOO TIKKIYA

**MAKES 12   PREPARATION TIME: 30 MINUTES
COOKING TIME: 25 MINUTES**

In India, these snacks, also called bread cutlets, are sold as street food.

200g/7oz **floury potatoes**, peeled and chopped

100g/3½oz/⅔ cup shelled **peas**, defrosted if frozen

3 slices **white bread**

1 **onion**, finely chopped

½ tsp **ground coriander**

¼ tsp **salt**

¼ tsp **chilli powder**

¼ tsp **ground cumin**

5cm/2in piece **root ginger**, peeled and grated

a few **coriander leaves**, finely chopped

4 tbsp **vegetable oil**

1 **BRING** a pan of water to the boil over a high heat. Add the potatoes and boil for 15 minutes, or until tender. Drain well and set aside. Meanwhile, bring another pan of water to the boil, add the peas and boil for 8–10 minutes until tender. Drain well, mash and set aside.

2 **SOAK** the bread in a bowl of cold water for 5 minutes while the vegetables are boiling.

3 **PREHEAT** the oven to low.

4 **SQUEEZE** out as much of the water from the bread as possible. Place it in a bowl with the potatoes, peas, onion, ground coriander, salt, chilli powder, cumin, ginger and coriander leaves and mix and mash together with a wooden spoon.

5 **WET** your hands slightly and roll the potato mixture into 12 balls of equal size, then flatten them until they are about 1cm/½in thick.

6 **HEAT** the oil in a frying pan over a medium heat. Add as many potato patties as will fit and fry them for about 4 minutes, turning once, until golden brown and crisp on both sides. Remove from the pan, drain well on kitchen paper and keep them warm in the oven while you fry the rest. These can be fried in advance and reheated in an oven at 180°C/350°F/Gas 4 for 10 minutes before serving. Serve hot.

VEGETABLE PATTIES *SABZI TIKKIYA*

**MAKES 8   PREPARATION TIME: 20 MINUTES
COOKING TIME: 25 MINUTES**

A tikki *is either chopped meat or vegetables with spices that are formed into a ball, pressed into a patty like a hamburger and then pan-fried.* Tikkiya, *the plural of tikki, are also often called cutlets.*

100g/3½oz **floury potatoes**, peeled and chopped

100g/3½oz/⅔ cup diced **carrots**

100g/3½oz/⅔ cup shelled **peas**, defrosted if frozen

2 **green chillies**, finely chopped

1 tsp freshly squeezed **lemon juice**

½ tsp **salt**

2 tbsp **rice flour**

about 2 tbsp **vegetable oil**

1 BRING a pan of water to the boil over a high heat. Add the potatoes and boil for 15 minutes, or until very tender, then drain well and set aside. Meanwhile, bring another pan of water to the boil, add the carrots and peas and boil for 8–10 minutes until tender, then drain well and set aside.

2 PREHEAT the oven to low.

3 MASH the potatoes and vegetables. Put them all in a bowl with the chillies, lemon juice and salt and mix until fairly smooth.

4 PUT the rice flour on a plate. Wet your hands slightly and roll the mashed potato mixture into 8 balls of equal size, then flatten them until they are about 3cm/1¼in thick. Coat them in the rice flour and set aside.

5 HEAT 2 tablespoons oil in a large frying pan over a medium heat. Add as many vegetable patties as will fit and fry them for about 4 minutes, turning once, until golden brown and crisp on both sides. Remove from the pan, drain well on kitchen paper and keep them warm in the oven. Fry the remaining patties in the same way, adding a little extra oil to the pan, if necessary. These can be fried in advance and reheated in an oven at 180°C/350°F/Gas 4 for 10 minutes before serving. Serve hot.

TOMATO SOUP

TAMATAR SHORBA

SERVES 4 PREPARATION TIME: 10 MINUTES
COOKING TIME: 25 MINUTES

This North Indian soup, created by cooking tomatoes with whole spices, is an aromatic recipe that's great in the winter as well as the summer.

2 tbsp groundnut oil, plus extra for drizzling

9 black peppercorns

2 bay leaves

1 cinnamon stick

2 garlic cloves, chopped

1 onion, chopped

600g/1lb 5oz tomatoes, chopped

2.5cm/1in piece root ginger, peeled and grated

2 tsp sugar

½ tsp salt

a pinch chilli powder (optional)

a pinch freshly ground black pepper

1 BRING 825ml/28fl oz/3⅓ cups water to the boil. Heat the oil in a large saucepan over a medium heat. Add the peppercorns, bay leaves and cinnamon and fry, stirring, for 30 seconds, or until you can smell the aroma of the spices. Watch carefully so they do not burn.

2 ADD the garlic and onion and continue stirring for 6–8 minutes until the onion is golden brown. Tip in the tomatoes and fry for a further 4–6 minutes until they are soft.

3 POUR in the boiling water, stir and return to the boil. Reduce the heat and simmer, uncovered, for 5 minutes, stirring occasionally.

4 ADD the ginger, sugar, salt and chilli powder, if using, and simmer for a further 5 minutes. Remove the cinnamon stick.

5 TRANSFER the soup to a blender and blend, then strain through a nylon sieve into the rinsed pan. Reheat gently and serve hot, drizzled with the extra peanut oil and sprinkled with the black pepper.

LENTIL SOUP *DAL SHORBA*

SERVES 4 PREPARATION TIME: 10 MINUTES
COOKING TIME: 25 MINUTES

Shorba (or shorva) is the Hindi word for soup. This spicy broth is made with red lentils, although you could just as easily use yellow lentils. Red lentils make a quicker-cooking version of the soup and are easier to digest.

125g/4oz/½ cup **split red lentils**

2 **green chillies**

15g/½oz **butter**

3 **black peppercorns**

1 **garlic** clove, chopped

½ tsp **salt**

a pinch **asafoetida**

1 BRING 625ml/21½fl oz/2½ cups water to the boil in a large saucepan over a high heat. Add the lentils and return the water to the boil. Partially cover the pan, reduce the heat to low and leave to simmer, stirring occasionally, for 15 minutes, or until the lentils become mushy. Watch carefully so the lentils don't burn. Top up with extra water, if necessary. Bring 125ml/4fl oz/½ cup water to the boil while the lentils finish simmering.

2 CUT off the chilli stalks and make a slit on each of the chillies; set aside.

3 MELT the butter in a small frying pan over a medium heat. Add the chillies, peppercorns, garlic, salt and asafoetida and let the spices sizzle for 30 seconds, or until you can smell the aroma. Watch carefully so they do not burn. Pour the mixture carefully into the lentils.

4 POUR over the boiling water and continue simmering, uncovered, for 5 minutes, or until the spices have blended into the lentils. Serve hot.

TANDOORI CHICKEN BITES

MURGH TIKKA

SERVES 4   PREPARATION TIME: 10 MINUTES, PLUS AT LEAST 2 HOURS
MARINATING TIME   COOKING TIME: 10–15 MINUTES

In India, these would be cooked in a tandoor, a clay oven with rounded sides and charcoal at the bottom. The meat prepared in a tandoor is generally moist and tender and has a special earthy aroma. In an ordinary domestic kitchen, however, these remain equally moist cooked in the oven or under a grill – or on a barbecue.

5cm/2in piece **root ginger**, peeled and grated

4 **garlic** cloves, crushed

4 tbsp **double cream**

2 tbsp **vegetable oil**, plus extra for brushing the oven shelf or grill rack

2 tbsp **natural yogurt**

1 tbsp **tomato purée**

1 tsp **Garam Masala** (*see page 23*)

1 tbsp **paprika**

1 tsp **ground cumin**

½ tsp **salt**

½ tsp **chilli powder**

500g/1lb 2oz boneless, skinless **chicken breasts**, chopped into bite-sized pieces

1 MIX all the ingredients, except the chicken pieces, together in a large bowl. Then add the chicken pieces and stir until they are well coated in the marinade.

2 COVER the bowl with cling film and refrigerate for at least 2 hours, or overnight.

3 PREHEAT the oven to 180°C/350°F/Gas 4, or heat the grill to medium.

4 SOAK 8 wooden skewers in cold water for 15 minutes, while the oven is heating.

5 THREAD the chicken on to the skewers, then place directly on to the oven shelves or under the grill and cook, turning and brushing with oil at least once, for 10–15 minutes, or until the chicken is cooked through. To check if the chicken is cooked, cut one piece – the juices should run clear. If not, cook for a few minutes more, then check again. Serve hot with Tomato, Onion and Chilli Salad (see page 160) and Coriander Chutney (see page 19).

CHILLI CHICKEN *MIRCH WALI MURGH*

**SERVES 4   PREPARATION TIME: 10 MINUTES
COOKING TIME: 12 MINUTES**

This spicy dish is a hybrid influenced by Chinese elements, and the piquant flavours of the soy sauce blend well with the sharpness of the turmeric and green chillies.

2 tbsp **soy sauce**

1 tbsp **tomato purée**

1 tbsp **tomato sauce**

1 tsp **chilli sauce**

1 tsp **malt vinegar**

1 tsp **sugar**

¼ tsp freshly ground **black pepper**

450g/1lb boneless, skinless **chicken breasts**, cut into strips

2 tbsp **cornflour**

½ tsp **turmeric**

¼ tsp **salt**

4 tbsp **groundnut** or **vegetable oil**

2 **garlic** cloves, chopped

1 **onion**, sliced, plus extra cut into rings, for serving

1 **green chilli**, chopped, plus extra sliced, for serving

1 STIR the soy sauce, tomato purée, tomato sauce, chilli sauce, vinegar, sugar and black pepper together in a small bowl, then set aside.

2 PUT the chicken strips in a large bowl with the cornflour, turmeric and salt and mix well.

3 HEAT the oil in a large frying pan or wok over a medium heat. Add the chicken pieces and fry, stirring occasionally, for 5 minutes, or until they change colour. Remove the chicken pieces from the pan with a slotted spoon and set aside.

4 TIP the garlic and onion into the oil remaining in the pan and fry, stirring, for 3 minutes.

5 ADD the green chilli and fry for 1 minute. Return the chicken pieces to the pan and fry for a further 1 minute.

6 STIR in the spicy sauce mixture and stir for 2 minutes, or until the chicken pieces are cooked through. Check by cutting into a piece of chicken – the juices should run clear. Serve hot topped with the onion rings and sliced green chillies.

MINCED LAMB KEBABS *SEEKH KEBABS*

MAKES **12**   PREPARATION TIME: **10** MINUTES, PLUS AT LEAST **2** HOURS MARINATING TIME   COOKING TIME: **10–15** MINUTES

The seekh kebab *is one of the best known tandoori dishes in Indian cooking. There are many recipes for these kebabs and each cook adds his or her own ingredients to give it a special flavour. Below is one of the most basic recipes, which uses a paste made of fried onions for a typical northern Indian sweetness. These are also ideal for cooking over a barbecue.*

500g/1lb 2oz **minced lamb**

5cm/2in piece **root ginger**, peeled and grated

4 **green chillies**, finely chopped

1 tsp **Garam Masala** (*see page 23*)

1 tsp **paprika**

½ tsp **salt**

4 tbsp **vegetable oil**, plus extra for brushing the grill rack

2 **onions**, finely chopped

1 SOAK 12 wooden skewers in cold water for 15 minutes. This prevents them burning when they are heated.

2 PUT the mince in a large bowl, add the ginger, chillies, garam masala, paprika and salt and mix well.

3 HEAT the oil in a large frying pan over a medium heat. Add the onions and fry, stirring occasionally, for 8–10 minutes until they are caramelized. Watch carefully so they do not burn.

4 PREHEAT the grill to high and lightly grease the grill rack, while the onions are frying.

5 ADD the onions to the minced lamb mixture and mix thoroughly.

6 DIVIDE the mixture into 12 equal portions. Wet your hands and shape each portion around a skewer, smoothing over the "seam".

7 PLACE the skewers under the grill and grill for 10–15 minutes, turning occasionally, until the meat is cooked through. These kebabs can be cooked in advance and warmed in an oven at 180°C/350°F/Gas 4 for 10 minutes before serving. Serve hot with Cucumber Relish (see page 22) and Tomato, Onion and Chilli Salad (see page 160).

DEEP-FRIED FISH *MACHCHI AMRITSARI*

MAKES ABOUT **24** PIECES   PREPARATION TIME: **10** MINUTES
COOKING TIME: **15–20** MINUTES

Amritsar, in Punjab in northern India, is steeped in history. These ajowan-laced fish fritters with a hint of chilli are a snack from that region. Any white fish, such as cod, halibut or coley, can be used to prepare them.

1 tsp **salt**

500g/1lb 2oz skinless **haddock fillets**, cut into bite-sized pieces

110g/3¾ oz/1 cup **chickpea** or **gram flour**

½ tsp **ground cumin**

½ tsp **ajowan seeds**

2.5cm/1in piece **root ginger**, peeled and grated

2 **garlic** cloves, finely chopped

2 **green chillies**, finely chopped

1 tbsp **malt vinegar**

vegetable oil for deep-frying

1 SPRINKLE ½ teaspoon salt over the fish and set aside.

2 PUT the remaining salt, the chickpea or gram flour, cumin and ajowan seeds in a large bowl and mix together. Stir in the ginger, garlic and chillies, then add the vinegar and 6 tablespoons water to make a thick, coarse batter. Add the fish to the batter and gently stir to make sure all the pieces are coated but don't break up.

3 HEAT enough oil for deep-frying in a heavy-based saucepan over a high heat or in a deep-fat fryer to 190ºC/375ºF, or until a small drop of batter sizzles fiercely in the oil. Place 1 piece of the fish in the oil and fry for 2 minutes, or until it is golden brown. Remove the fish from the oil with a slotted spoon and drain on kitchen paper. Taste the fish and adjust the seasoning of the batter, adding more salt, if necessary.

4 FRY the remaining pieces of fish, working in batches to avoid overcrowding the pan, if necessary. Remove any pieces of fried batter from the oil and return the oil to the correct temperature before adding each new batch. These can be fried in advance and reheated in an oven at 180ºC/350ºF/Gas 4 for 10 minutes before serving. Serve hot with Coriander Chutney (see page 19).

PRAWN FRITTERS *JHINGA PAKORAS*

**MAKES 24   PREPARATION TIME: 15 MINUTES
COOKING TIME: 15–20 MINUTES**

These are heavenly, golden, mini clusters of prawns in a spicy, crispy batter.

¼ tsp **turmeric**

¼ tsp **salt**

250g/9oz peeled and cooked **prawns**

2.5cm/1in piece **root ginger**, peeled
and finely chopped

4 **garlic** cloves, chopped

1 **onion**, finely chopped

110g/3¾oz/1 cup **chickpea** or **gram flour**

½ tsp **ground cumin**

¼ tsp **chilli powder**

vegetable oil for deep-frying

1 SPRINKLE the turmeric and salt over the prawns and set aside.

2 PUT the ginger, garlic and onion in a large bowl, then stir in the flour, cumin and chilli powder.

3 POUR in 100ml/3½fl oz/scant ½ cup water and mix with a fork until a thick batter forms. If it appears runny, add a little extra flour, then stir in the prawns.

4 HEAT enough oil for deep-frying in a heavy-based saucepan over a high heat or in a deep-fat fryer to 190°C/375°, or until a small drop of the batter sizzles fiercely in the oil.

5 DROP 1 tablespoon of the batter into the oil and fry for 1 minute, or until it turns golden brown.

6 REMOVE the fritter from the oil with a slotted spoon and drain on kitchen paper. Allow to cool for 1 minute, then taste the fritter and adjust the seasoning of the batter, adding more salt, if necessary.

7 FRY the remaining fritters, working in batches to avoid overcrowding the pan, if necessary. Remove any pieces of fried batter from the oil and return the oil to the correct temperature before adding each new batch. These can be fried in advance and reheated in an oven at 180°C/350°F/ Gas 4 for 10 minutes. Serve hot.

PRAWN POORIS *JHINGA POORIS*

SERVES 4   PREPARATION TIME: 10 MINUTES, PLUS MAKING THE POORIS
COOKING TIME: 20 MINUTES

This spicy prawn dish with deep-fried breads is very likely influenced by the foods of West Bengal and Bangladesh.

300g/10½oz peeled **king prawns**

¼ tsp **turmeric**

¼ tsp **salt**

3 tbsp **groundnut** or **vegetable oil**

2.5cm/1in piece **root ginger**, peeled and chopped

2 **green chillies**, chopped

2 **garlic** cloves, chopped

1 **onion**, chopped

2 **tomatoes**, chopped

2 tsp **tomato purée**

2 tsp **sugar**

½ tsp **ground coriander**

½ tsp **ground cumin**

½ tsp **paprika**

1 tsp **malt vinegar**

1 recipe quantity **Pooris** (*see page 30*), cooked and reheated, to serve

1 PLACE the prawns in a large bowl and sprinkle over the turmeric and salt, then set aside.

2 HEAT the oil in a saucepan or wok over a medium heat. Add the ginger, chillies, garlic and onion and fry, stirring frequently, for 6–8 minutes until the onion is golden brown.

3 STIR in the tomatoes, tomato purée, sugar, coriander, cumin and paprika. Reduce the heat to medium-low and simmer, stirring often, for 5 minutes, or until the sauce turns dark red.

4 TIP in the marinated prawns and the vinegar and cook for a further 3 minutes, or until the mixture becomes quite thick and droplets of oil are visible on the surface. Serve the prawn mixture hot, allowing 2 pooris per person. The pooris can be made several hours in advance and reheated in an oven at 180°C/350°F/Gas 4 for 5 minutes before serving.

CHICKPEA CURRY *CHANNA MASALA*

SERVES **4**   PREPARATION TIME: **15** MINUTES
COOKING TIME: **25** MINUTES

This spicy and tangy Punjabi recipe uses brewed tea to darken the gravy.

1 **tea bag**

6 tbsp **vegetable oil**

2 **bay leaves**

5–6cm/2–2½in piece **cassia bark**
or **cinnamon stick**

2 **onions**, finely chopped

5cm/2in piece **root ginger**, peeled and chopped

6 **garlic** cloves

1 tsp **ground cumin**

1 tsp **ground coriander**

½ tsp **turmeric**

½ tsp **salt**

¼ tsp **mango powder**

¼ tsp **chilli powder**

¼ tsp **ground pomegranate seeds**

¼ tsp **Garam Masala** (*see page 23*)

2 cans (400g/14oz each) **chickpeas**, drained
and rinsed

1 BRING 500ml/17fl oz/2 cups water to the boil. Put the tea bag in a heatproof bowl, pour over the boiling water and set aside to brew.

2 HEAT the oil in a large saucepan over a medium heat. Add the bay leaves and the cassia bark or cinnamon and fry, stirring constantly, for 30 seconds, or until they splutter. Watch carefully, so they do not burn.

3 ADD the onions and fry, stirring frequently, for 6–8 minutes until they are golden brown.

4 PUT the ginger and garlic in a blender and blend together until a coarse paste forms. Add to the pan with the cumin, coriander, turmeric, salt, mango powder, chilli powder, ground pomegranate seeds and garam masala and continue stirring for 2 minutes.

5 TIP in the chickpeas and continue stirring for a further 5 minutes, mashing some of the chickpeas against the side of the pan with a wooden spoon.

6 DISCARD the tea bag and stir the tea into the pan. Leave the mixture to simmer for 7–8 minutes, stirring occasionally, until it becomes quite thick. Serve with Chapatis (see page 29) and Coriander Chutney (see page 19).

FRIED PULSES *BHUNA DAL*

SERVES 4   PREPARATION TIME: 10 MINUTES, PLUS 1 HOUR SOAKING TIME
COOKING TIME: 30–40 MINUTES

60g/2¼oz/¼ cup **split yellow lentils**

60g/2¼oz/¼ cup **split red lentils**

60g/2¼oz/¼ cup **split dried mung beans**

60g/2¼oz/¼ cup **split Bengal gram**

70g/2½oz **butter** or **ghee**

a pinch **asafoetida**

4 **garlic** cloves, finely chopped

1 **onion**, finely chopped

¼ tsp **salt**

¼ tsp **turmeric**

¼ tsp **chilli powder**

¼ tsp **Garam Masala** (*see page 23*)

½ tsp **brown** or **black mustard seeds**

¼ tsp **cumin seeds**

5cm/2in piece **root ginger**, peeled and grated

8 **curry leaves**

2 **green chillies**, chopped

1 PLACE the lentils, mung beans and Bengal gram in a bowl, cover with cold water and leave to soak for 1 hour.

2 BRING 1 litre/35fl oz/4 cups water to the boil when the pulses have almost finished soaking. Drain the pulses, then place them in a large saucepan over a high heat. Pour over the boiling water and return the water to the boil. Partially cover the pan, reduce the heat to low and leave to simmer, stirring occasionally, for 20–30 minutes until yellow and mushy. Watch carefully so the pulses do not burn. Top up with extra water, if necessary.

3 MELT 50g/1¾oz of the butter or ghee in a separate pan over a medium heat. Stir in the asafoetida, garlic and onion and fry, stirring frequently, for 6–8 minutes until the onion is golden brown. Stir in the salt, turmeric and chilli powder, then add the pulses with any remaining cooking water and simmer, uncovered, stirring occasionally, for 10 minutes. Sprinkle with the garam masala.

4 MELT the remaining butter in a small frying pan over a medium heat. Add the mustard and cumin seeds and stir for about 30 seconds until they begin to splutter. Watch carefully so they do not burn. Stir in the ginger, curry leaves and chillies and stir a further 30 seconds.

5 POUR the spice mixture over the lentils. Serve hot.

KIDNEY BEANS IN SPICY TOMATO AND GARLIC GRAVY *RAJMAH LABABDAR*

**SERVES 4   PREPARATION TIME: 15 MINUTES
COOKING TIME: 25–30 MINUTES**

Particularly popular in Kashmir and Punjab, this hearty dish tastes even better the day after it is made.

3 tbsp **vegetable oil**

1 tsp **cumin seeds**

4 **garlic** cloves, chopped

1 **onion**, chopped

3 **tomatoes**, chopped

2.5cm/1in piece **root ginger**, peeled and grated

¼ tsp **chilli powder**

¼ tsp **ground ginger**

2 cans (400g/14oz each) **red kidney beans**, drained and rinsed

15g/½oz **butter**

¼ tsp **salt**

¼ tsp **Garam Masala** (*see page 23*)

a few **coriander leaves**, roughly chopped

1 **HEAT** the oil in a large saucepan over a medium heat. Add the cumin seeds and fry, stirring, for 30 seconds, or until they splutter. Watch carefully so they do not burn.

2 **ADD** the garlic and onion and fry, stirring frequently, for 6–8 minutes until the onion is golden brown. Bring 350ml/12fl oz/1½ cups water to the boil while the onion fries.

3 **TIP** the tomatoes into the pan and continue frying, stirring occasionally, for 5 minutes. Add the root ginger, chilli powder and ground ginger and continue stirring for a further 1 minute. Stir in the kidney beans.

4 **POUR** over half the boiling water and add the butter. Use a wooden spoon to mash a few of the beans against the side of the pan, then leave the mixture to simmer for 4–5 minutes. Add the remaining boiling water and continue to simmer, uncovered, for 7 minutes, stirring occasionally, until the mixture thickens.

5 **STIR** in the salt and garam masala and serve hot, sprinkled with the coriander leaves.

VEGETABLE DHANSAK *PARSI DHANSAK*

SERVES 4 PREPARATION TIME: 10 MINUTES
COOKING TIME: 50–55 MINUTES

A dhansak is a spiced dish of puréed lentils and vegetables cooked in a tangy sauce. This is a Parsi recipe that comes from western India.

100g/3½oz/scant ½ cup **split yellow lentils**

100g/3½oz/scant ½ cup **split dried yellow mung beans**

200g/7oz **floury potatoes**, peeled and quartered

200g/7oz **carrots**, chopped

115g/4oz **butter** or **ghee**

5cm/2in piece **root ginger**, peeled and chopped

4 **garlic** cloves, chopped

3 **green chillies**, chopped

2 **onions**, chopped

1 tbsp **Dhansak Masala** (*see page 24*)

½ tsp **turmeric**

½ tsp **salt**

2 **tomatoes**, finely chopped

1 BRING 750ml/26fl oz/3 cups water to the boil over a high heat. Add the lentils and mung beans and return the water to the boil. Partially cover the pan, reduce the heat to low and leave to simmer, stirring occasionally, for 35–40 minutes until the mixture becomes mushy. Watch carefully so the mixture does not burn. Top up with extra boiling water, if necessary.

2 BRING another large saucepan of water to the boil over a high heat while the lentils are simmering. Add the potatoes and carrots, return the water to the boil and boil for 20–25 minutes until they are both very tender and the potatoes almost falling apart, then drain well.

3 POUR the lentils and any remaining water into a blender. Add the drained potatoes and carrots and blend until the mixture forms a thick purée. Set aside.

4 MELT the butter or ghee in a large saucepan over a medium-low heat. Add the ginger, garlic, chillies and onions and fry, stirring occasionally, for 10 minutes, or until the onions are caramelized.

5 STIR in the dhansak masala, turmeric and salt, then add the tomatoes and cook for 1 minute, stirring occasionally. Stir in the lentil and vegetable mixture and continue stirring for 2 minutes, then serve.

BUTTERY SPINACH AND POTATOES

SAAG ALOO

SERVES **4** PREPARATION TIME: **15** MINUTES
COOKING TIME: **25** MINUTES

This popular vegetarian dish, served in Indian restaurants around the world, can be made with spinach or mustard leaves. If the fresh spinach in this recipe is unavailable or out of season, replace it with frozen chopped spinach, defrosting it before you add it to the pan.

60g/2¼oz **butter** or **ghee**

5cm/2in piece **root ginger**, peeled and grated

4 **garlic** cloves, chopped

2 **onions**, chopped

2 **green chillies**, chopped

200g/7oz **floury potatoes**, peeled and cut into 5cm/2in cubes

1 tsp **ground cumin**

1 tsp **ground coriander**

½ tsp **turmeric**

¼ tsp **salt**

500g/1lb 2oz **spinach leaves**, rinsed and chopped

a pinch **Garam Masala** (*see page 23*)

1 MELT the butter or ghee in a large saucepan over a medium heat. Add the ginger, garlic, onions and chillies and fry, stirring frequently, for 2 minutes.

2 ADD the potatoes and continue stirring for 5 minutes.

3 TIP in the cumin, coriander, turmeric and salt, followed by the spinach with just the water clinging to the leaves and continue frying and stirring for 15 minutes, or until the potatoes are tender.

4 SPRINKLE the garam masala over and serve hot with Chickpea Curry (see page 62) and Chapatis (see page 29).

POTATOES WITH CAULIFLOWER

ALOO GOBHI MASALA

SERVES 4 PREPARATION TIME: 15 MINUTES
COOKING TIME: 25 MINUTES

In India, cauliflower is harvested during the winter months. The nation ranks second in the production of this vegetable, so this recipe is extremely popular. It is usually featured in dishes that contain little gravy and is often served alongside a lentil dish.

4 tbsp **vegetable oil**

1 tsp **brown mustard seeds**

600g/1lb 5oz **waxy potatoes**, peeled and cut into 2.5cm/1in pieces

2.5cm/1in piece **root ginger**, peeled and chopped

4 **garlic** cloves, chopped

2 **green chillies**, chopped

1 **onion**, chopped

1 tsp **turmeric**

1 tsp **ground cumin**

½ tsp **salt**

600g/1lb 5oz **cauliflower** florets

¼ tsp **Garam Masala** (*see page 23*)

a few **coriander leaves**, roughly chopped

1 **HEAT** the oil in a saucepan over a medium heat. Add the mustard seeds and stir for 30 seconds, or until the seeds start to splutter. Watch carefully so they do not burn.

2 **TIP** the potatoes into the pan and increase the heat to medium-high. Continue stirring for 6 minutes, or until the edges brown. Bring 310ml/10¾fl oz/1¼ cups water to the boil, while the potatoes cook.

3 **ADD** the ginger, garlic, chillies and onion to the potatoes and continue frying, stirring frequently, for 5 minutes. Add the turmeric, ground cumin and salt, followed by the cauliflower. Continue frying, stirring occasionally, for 3 minutes. Pour in the boiling water and stir well.

4 **COVER** the pan and leave the mixture to simmer for 9–10 minutes until the potatoes and cauliflower are tender.

5 **STIR** in the garam masala and sprinkle with the coriander. Serve hot with Chapatis (see page 29).

SWEET POTATO CURRY

SHAKARKAND KI CURRY

SERVES 4   PREPARATION TIME: 10 MINUTES
COOKING TIME: 15 MINUTES

Many Hindus eat sweet potatoes during religious festivals in the summer when the tubers are simply baked or boiled. At other times they are used in more flavoursome preparations such as this one.

600g/1lb 5oz **sweet potatoes**, peeled and cut into bite-sized chunks

½ tsp **salt**

2 tbsp **vegetable oil**

1 **green chilli**, chopped

½ tsp **cumin seeds**

a few chopped **coriander leaves**

1 BRING 600ml/21½fl oz/2½ cups water to the boil in a large saucepan over a high heat. Add the sweet potatoes and ¼ teaspoon of the salt and return the water to the boil, then reduce the heat and leave the sweet potatoes to simmer for 10 minutes, or until tender when pierced with the tip of a knife.

2 DRAIN the sweet potatoes well, carefully shaking off any excess water, then set aside.

3 HEAT the oil in a large frying pan or wok over a medium heat. Add the chilli and cumin seeds and fry for 30 seconds, stirring, or until the seeds splutter. Watch carefully so the spices do not burn.

4 TIP in the sweet potatoes and the remaining ¼ teaspoon salt and stir for 2 minutes until well combined and the sweet potatoes are hot.

5 SPRINKLE with the coriander leaves and serve hot.

MIXED VEGETABLE CURRY

HARA MASALA SABZI

SERVES 4   PREPARATION TIME: 10 MINUTES
COOKING TIME: 20 MINUTES

Vegetables have always been an extremely important part of the diet of all Indians, and many Indians are strict vegetarians for religious reasons.

150g/5½oz **carrots**, cut into batons

100g/3½oz/⅔ cup shelled **peas**, defrosted if frozen

100g/3½oz/⅔ cup **sweetcorn**, defrosted if frozen

200g/7oz **broccoli** florets

1 **red pepper**, cut into chunks

3 tbsp **vegetable oil**

1 recipe quantity **Green Masala Paste**
   (*see page 25*)

¼ tsp **salt**

1 **BRING** 500ml/17fl oz/2 cups water to the boil in a large saucepan over a high heat. Add the carrots, peas and sweetcorn and boil for 5 minutes. Add the broccoli and red pepper and continue boiling for a further 5 minutes. Drain the vegetables and set aside.

2 **HEAT** the oil in a large saucepan or wok over a medium heat while the vegetables are cooking. Add the green masala paste and salt and fry, stirring constantly, for 3 minutes. Watch carefully so the mixture does not brown too much.

3 **ADD** the vegetables to the pan and stir. Continue frying, stirring to combine the ingredients, for 3 minutes. Bring 250ml/9fl oz/1 cup water to the boil, while the vegetables are frying.

4 **POUR** over the boiling water and continue simmering for a further 1 minute, or until droplets of oil appear on the surface. Serve hot with Plain Basmati Rice (see page 31).

PANEER WITH PEAS *MATTAR PANEER*

SERVES 4   PREPARATION TIME: 10 MINUTES
COOKING TIME: 20–25 MINUTES

This dish is eaten all over northern India, practically on a daily basis.

3 tomatoes, roughly chopped

5 tbsp vegetable oil

500g/1lb 2oz paneer, cut into bite-sized cubes

2 tsp cumin seeds

2.5cm/1in piece root ginger, peeled and chopped

6 garlic cloves, chopped

2 onions, chopped

¼ tsp turmeric

¼ tsp chilli powder

½ tsp salt

250g/9oz/1⅔ cups shelled peas, defrosted if frozen

¼ tsp Garam Masala (*see page 23*)

3 tbsp double cream

a few coriander leaves, roughly chopped

1 TIP the tomatoes and their juice into a blender and blend until smooth, then set aside.

2 HEAT the oil in a wok or saucepan over a medium heat. Add the paneer and fry for about 4 minutes, gently turning occasionally, until the edges are browned. Remove with a slotted spoon and set aside.

3 ADD the cumin seeds to the oil remaining in the pan and fry, stirring constantly, for 30 seconds or until the seeds splutter. Watch carefully so they do not burn. Add the ginger, garlic and onions and fry, stirring frequently, for 6–8 minutes until the onions are golden brown, then stir in the turmeric, chilli powder and salt. Bring 310ml/10¾fl oz/1¼ cups water to the boil while the onions are frying.

4 TIP the peas into the pan and continue stirring for 2 minutes. Add the blended tomatoes and simmer for a further 3 minutes.

5 RETURN the paneer to the pan and add the boiling water. Stir well and leave to simmer, uncovered, for 5 minutes, or until droplets of oil appear on the surface.

6 SPRINKLE with the garam masala, swirl in the cream and scatter over the coriander leaves. Serve hot.

REGAL PANEER *SHAHI PANEER*

SERVES 4   PREPARATION TIME: 15 MINUTES   COOKING TIME: 15 MINUTES

The Moghul influence of using dairy products in cooking is obvious in dishes like this from Hyderabad. This is a deliciously piquant, hot and creamy curry.

200g/7oz **plum tomatoes**, coarsely chopped

1 tbsp **cornflour**

3 tbsp **vegetable oil**

2 **black cardamom pods**

1 tsp **cumin seeds**

4 **garlic** cloves, crushed

2 **green chillies**, finely chopped

1 **onion**, finely chopped

2 tbsp **natural yogurt**, whisked

1 tbsp **tomato purée**

1 tsp **sugar**

½ tsp **salt**

a pinch **chilli powder**

500g/1lb 2oz **paneer**, cut into bite-sized cubes

5cm/2in piece **root ginger**, peeled and grated

2 tbsp **double cream**

a pinch **Garam Masala** (*see page 23*)

a few **coriander leaves**

1 **TIP** the tomatoes and their juice into a blender and blend until smooth, then set aside. Put the cornflour in a small bowl and stir in 2 tablespoons water to make a smooth paste, then set aside.

2 **HEAT** the oil in a large saucepan over a medium heat. Add the cardamom pods and cumin seeds and fry for 30 seconds, stirring constantly, or until they splutter. Watch carefully so they do not burn.

3 **ADD** the garlic, chillies and onion and continue frying, stirring frequently, for 6–8 minutes until the onion turns golden brown.

4 **TIP** in the tomatoes and simmer, uncovered, for 4 minutes, or until the sauce becomes thick.

5 **STIR** in the yogurt, followed by the cornflour paste. Add the tomato purée, sugar, salt, chilli powder and 4 tablespoons cold water and bring to the boil, stirring.

6 **REDUCE** the heat to low. Add the paneer and gently stir it into the gravy. Leave the mixture to simmer, uncovered, for 2–3 minutes, until droplets of oil appear on the surface. Stir in the ginger.

7 **SWIRL** in the cream and sprinkle with the garam masala. Tear the coriander leaves and scatter over the paneer, then serve.

VEGETABLE BIRYANI *SABZ BIRYANI*

SERVES 4   PREPARATION TIME: 20 MINUTES   COOKING TIME: 40 MINUTES

75g/2½oz **butter** or **ghee**, plus extra for greasing

1 **onion**, sliced

2 x 5cm/2in pieces **cassia bark**

6 **green cardamom pods**

4 **cloves**

2 **bay leaves**

1 tsp **cumin seeds**

150g/5½oz **carrots**, cut into batons

100g/3½oz/⅔ cup shelled **peas**, defrosted if frozen

100g/3½oz/⅔ cup **sweetcorn**, defrosted if frozen

200g/7oz **broccoli** florets

1 **red pepper**, cut into chunks

8 **cashew nuts**

250ml/9fl oz/1 cup **natural yogurt**, whisked

6 **garlic** cloves

½ tsp **Garam Masala** (*see page 23*)

½ tsp **chilli powder**

½ tsp **salt**

1 recipe quantity **Plain Basmati Rice** (*see page 31*), cooked

10 **saffron strands**

1 MELT the butter or ghee in a large saucepan over a medium heat. Add the onion and fry, stirring occasionally, for 6–8 minutes until it is golden brown. Remove the onion from the pan and set aside.

2 INCREASE the heat to medium-high. Add the cassia bark, green cardamom pods, cloves, bay leaves and cumin seeds to the butter or ghee left in the pan and fry for 30 seconds, stirring, or until you can smell the aroma.

3 TIP in the vegetables and cashew nuts and continue frying for 5 minutes, stirring occasionally, or until the nuts are golden brown.

4 PREHEAT the oven to 180°C/350°F/Gas 4. Grease a large ovenproof casserole with a tight-fitting lid.

5 PUT the onion in a blender. Add the yogurt, garlic, garam masala, chilli powder and salt and blend until smooth. Stir this mixture into the vegetables.

6 PLACE a layer of vegetables on the base of the casserole and cover it with a layer of the cooked rice and a few saffron strands.

7 REPEAT these layers until all the ingredients have been used, ending with a layer of rice. Cover and bake for 25 minutes, or until the biryani is heated through. Serve hot with Cucumber Relish (see page 22).

CHICKEN TIKKA MASALA

MURGH TIKKA MASALA

SERVES 4   PREPARATION TIME: 15 MINUTES, PLUS AT LEAST 2 HOURS
MARINATING TIME   COOKING TIME: 15–20 MINUTES

*Now said to be the world's most popular Indian dish, this actually originated
from the kitchens of Bangladeshi chefs in the UK.*

4 **tomatoes**, chopped

6 tbsp **double cream**

5cm/2in piece **root ginger**, peeled and grated

4 **garlic** cloves, chopped

3 tbsp **vegetable oil**

2 **bay leaves**

2 **onions**, finely chopped

2 **green chillies**, finely chopped

1 tsp **ground cumin**

1 tsp **ground coriander**

½ tsp **paprika**

¼ tsp **turmeric**

¼ tsp **salt**

a pinch **Garam Masala** (*see page 23*)

1 recipe quantity **Tandoori Chicken Bites**
   (*see page 51*), cooked

1 **PLACE** the tomatoes, cream, ginger and garlic in a blender and blend
until a thick sauce forms, then set aside.

2 **HEAT** the oil in a large saucepan with a tight-fitting lid over a medium
heat. Add the bay leaves and onions and fry, stirring constantly, for
6–8 minutes until the onions are golden brown.

3 **ADD** the chillies, cumin, coriander, paprika, turmeric, salt and garam
masala and stir for 1 minute, or until you can smell the aroma of the
spices. Watch carefully so the mixture does not burn.

4 **TIP** in the chicken pieces and fry, stirring occasionally, 3 minutes.
Stir the tomato and cream mixture into the pan, cover, and reduce
the heat to low. Simmer 5 minutes until the chicken is heated through.

5 **BRING** 125ml/4fl oz/½ cup water to the boil while the chicken mixture
is simmering, then add the boiling water to the chicken and simmer
for a further 1 minute, stirring, or until droplets of oil appear on the
surface. Serve hot with Buttery Spinach and Potatoes (*see page 70*)
and Plain Basmati Rice (*see page 31*).

CHICKEN BREASTS MARINATED IN PICKLING SPICES *ACHAARI MURGH*

SERVES 4 PREPARATION TIME: 10 MINUTES
COOKING TIME: 25–30 MINUTES

This North Indian dish is prepared with many of the whole spices traditionally used to make pickles. Mustard oil is often used in this spicy curry to give it a headier flavour, but milder-tasting vegetable oil is used here.

4 tbsp **vegetable oil**

4 **dried red chillies**

½ tsp **brown mustard seeds**

½ tsp **fenugreek seeds**

½ tsp **cumin seeds**

½ tsp **nigella seeds**

½ tsp **fennel seeds**

2 **onions**, chopped

5cm/2in piece **root ginger**, peeled and grated

6 **garlic** cloves, finely chopped

½ tsp **turmeric**

500g/1lb 2oz boneless, skinless **chicken breasts**, chopped into bite-sized pieces

250ml/9fl oz/1 cup **natural yogurt**, whisked

1 tsp freshly squeezed **lemon juice**

1 **HEAT** the oil in a saucepan with a tight-fitting lid over a medium-high heat. Add the chillies and the mustard, fenugreek, cumin, nigella and fennel seeds and fry, stirring constantly, for 30 seconds, or until the seeds splutter. Watch carefully so they do not burn.

2 **TIP** in the onions and fry, stirring, for 6–8 minutes until they are golden brown. Stir in the ginger, garlic and turmeric.

3 **ADD** the chicken pieces and continue frying for a further 8–10 minutes until the chicken colours on the outside. Bring 185ml/6fl oz/¾ cup water to the boil while the chicken cooks.

4 **STIR** in the yogurt, followed by the boiling water. Cover the pan, reduce the heat to low and leave the mixture to simmer for 5 minutes, or until the chicken is cooked through. Check by cutting a piece of chicken in half – the juices should run clear.

5 **SPRINKLE** over the lemon juice and simmer for a further 2 minutes, or until droplets of oil appear on the surface. Serve hot.

BUTTER CHICKEN *MURGH MAKHANI*

SERVES 4   PREPARATION TIME: 20 MINUTES, PLUS AT LEAST 30 MINUTES
MARINATING TIME   COOKING TIME: 20–25 MINUTES

100g/3½oz peeled **plum tomatoes** *(see page 18)*

4 **garlic** cloves, crushed

2 tbsp **natural yogurt**

2 tbsp **double cream**

½ tsp freshly ground **black pepper**

½ tsp **paprika**

¼ tsp **chilli powder**

a large pinch **ground cinnamon**

4 tbsp **vegetable oil**

500g/1lb 2oz boneless, skinless **chicken breasts**, cut into bite-sized pieces

2 **onions**, finely chopped

¼ tsp **salt**

¼ tsp **ground fenugreek**

15g/½oz **butter**

¼ tsp **Garam Masala** *(see page 23)*

a few **coriander leaves**

1 TIP the tomatoes into a blender and blend until smooth, then set aside.

2 PUT the garlic, yogurt, cream, black pepper, paprika, chilli powder, cinnamon and 1 tablespoon of the oil in a large bowl and stir well. Add the chicken pieces to this marinade and stir until well coated. Cover the bowl with cling film and refrigerate for at least 30 minutes, or overnight, to let the flavours blend.

3 HEAT the remaining 3 tablespoons oil in a large saucepan or wok over a medium heat. Add the onions and fry, stirring occasionally, for 6–8 minutes until golden brown. Add the salt and fenugreek and continue frying for a further 1 minute until you can smell the aroma.

4 TIP in the tomatoes and continue stirring for 3 minutes, or until the mixture becomes quite thick.

5 STIR in the butter, add the chicken and the marinade and reduce the heat to low. Simmer, uncovered, for 10 minutes, stirring occasionally, or until the chicken is cooked through. Check by cutting a piece of chicken in half – the juices should run clear. Sprinkle over the garam masala and coriander leaves and serve hot with Naans (see page 26).

CHICKEN DHANSAK *MURGH DHANSAK*

SERVES 4   PREPARATION TIME: 10 MINUTES, PLUS BOILING THE POTATOES
AND CARROTS   COOKING TIME: 1 HOUR 20 MINUTES

100g/3½oz/scant ½ cup **split Bengal gram**

150g/5½oz **green beans**, topped, tailed and chopped

150g/5½oz **carrots**, peeled and chopped

80g/2¾oz **butter** or **ghee**

5cm/2in piece **root ginger**, chopped

4 **garlic** cloves, chopped

3 **green chillies**, chopped

2 **onions**, chopped

4 tsp **Dhansak Masala** *(see page 24)*

½ tsp **turmeric**

½ tsp **salt**

500g/1lb 2oz boneless, skinless **chicken breasts**, cut into bite-sized pieces

2 tsp **tomato purée**

1 **BRING** 375ml/13fl oz/1½ cups water to the boil over a high heat. Add the Bengal gram and return the water to the boil. Partially cover the pan, reduce the heat to low and simmer, stirring occasionally, for 55 minutes, or until the mixture becomes mushy. Watch carefully so it does not burn. Top up with extra boiling water, if necessary.

2 **BRING** another large saucepan of water to the boil over a high heat while the Bengal gram is simmering. Add the green beans and carrots and boil for 10–15 minutes until they are both soft, then drain well.

3 **POUR** the Bengal gram and any remaining water into a blender. Add the green beans and carrots and blend until smooth; set aside.

4 **MELT** the butter or ghee in a large saucepan over a medium heat, then add the ginger, garlic, chillies and onions. Fry, stirring frequently, for 6–8 minutes until the onions are golden brown. Add the dhansak masala, turmeric and salt to the onions and stir for 30 seconds. Bring 300ml/10½fl oz/1¼ cups water to the boil.

5 **TIP** in the chicken and continue cooking, stirring, for 5 minutes, or until the chicken changes colour. Pour in the boiling water, stir in the tomato purée and simmer for a further 1 minute, stirring.

6 **STIR** in the Bengal gram and vegetable mixture, then simmer for 5–7 minutes, stirring occasionally, until the chicken is cooked through. Check by cutting a piece of chicken in half – the juices should run clear. Serve hot.

CHICKEN WITH CARAMELIZED ONION, GARLIC AND GINGER

MURGH MASALA

SERVES 4   PREPARATION TIME: 10 MINUTES
COOKING TIME: 25–30 MINUTES

Onions, garlic, ginger, chilli and tomato form the foundation of many curries.

4 **tomatoes**, coarsely chopped

100g/3½oz **butter** or **ghee**

5cm/2in piece **cinnamon stick**

4 **cloves**

2 **onions**, finely chopped

4 **garlic** cloves, chopped

1 tsp **ground cumin**

1 tsp **ground coriander**

¼ tsp **turmeric**

¼ tsp **chilli powder**

¼ tsp **salt**

500g/1lb 2oz boneless, skinless **chicken breasts**, cut into bite-sized pieces

5cm/2in piece **root ginger**, peeled and grated

¼ tsp **Garam Masala** (*see page 23*)

1 **TIP** the tomatoes into a blender and blend until smooth, then set aside.

2 **MELT** the butter or ghee in a saucepan or wok over a medium heat. Add the cinnamon and cloves and fry, stirring, for 30 seconds, or until you can smell the aroma of the spices. Watch carefully so they do not burn.

3 **ADD** the onions and garlic and fry, stirring frequently, for 6–8 minutes until they are golden brown. Add the cumin, coriander, turmeric, chilli powder and salt and stir for 1 minute.

4 **STIR** in the chicken and continue frying, stirring, for 7–8 minutes until the chicken colours. Bring 6½ tablespoons water to the boil while the chicken is cooking.

5 **ADD** the tomatoes, followed by the boiling water, to the chicken and simmer for 10–15 minutes until droplets of oil appear on the surface.

6 **STIR** in the ginger and garam masala and stir in. Serve hot with Cucumber Relish (see page 22) and Chapatis (see page 29).

GRIDDLED CHICKEN *MURGH TAKA TAK*

SERVES 4 PREPARATION TIME: 10 MINUTES
COOKING TIME: ABOUT 15 MINUTES

This dish gets its Indian name from the sound of the spoon or spatula hitting the pan and breaking up the food while it cooks – taka tak is the rhythm of chopping the chicken pieces as they cook in the pan over a high heat.

4 tbsp **vegetable oil**

1 tsp **cumin seeds**

2 **onions**, sliced

2.5cm/1in piece **root ginger**, peeled and grated

6 **garlic** cloves, crushed

3 **green chillies**, chopped

500g/1lb 2oz boneless, skinless **chicken breasts**, cut into bite-sized pieces

2 **tomatoes**, chopped

½ tsp **salt**

¼ tsp **turmeric**

a pinch **Garam Masala** (*see page 23*)

a handful **fenugreek leaves**

1 **HEAT** the oil in a large frying pan or wok over a medium heat, then add the cumin seeds and fry, stirring constantly, for 30 seconds, or until they splutter. Watch carefully so they do not burn. Add the onions and continue frying, stirring, for 3 minutes until the onions start to soften.

2 **ADD** the ginger, garlic and chillies and continue frying for 2 minutes, or until all the spices are blended.

3 **TIP** in the chicken and fry for 4 minutes, breaking the chicken into smaller pieces against the side of the pan with a spatula or wooden spoon, until the chicken changes colour.

4 **ADD** the tomatoes, salt, turmeric and garam masala and continue frying, stirring, for 4 minutes.

5 **STIR** in the fenugreek leaves and fry for a further 5 minutes until all the chicken pieces are cooked through. Check by cutting a piece of chicken in half – the juices should run clear. Serve hot with Cucumber Relish (see page 22) and Naans (see page 26).

CHICKEN JALFREZI *MURGH JALFREZI*

SERVES 4 PREPARATION TIME: 10 MINUTES
COOKING TIME: 20–25 MINUTES

Jalfrezi is a dish in which meat or vegetables are fried in oil and spices to produce a thick, dry gravy. Peppers, onions and fresh green chillies are then added to make a moderately hot curry.

3 tbsp **vegetable oil**

2 **onions**, chopped

4 **garlic** cloves, sliced

2 **green chillies**, chopped

4 tsp **Manju's Quick Curry Paste**
   (*see page 24*)

1 tsp **tomato purée**

¼ tsp **salt**

500g/1lb 2oz boneless, skinless **chicken breasts**, chopped into bite-sized pieces

5cm/2in piece **root ginger**, peeled and grated

2 **green peppers**, seeded and sliced

1 HEAT the oil in a large saucepan over a medium heat. Add the onions, garlic and chillies and fry, stirring frequently, for 6–8 minutes until the onions are golden brown.

2 ADD the curry paste, tomato purée and salt and stir for 1 minute. Stir in the chicken pieces and continue stirring for 7–8 minutes until they change colour and the spices blend with the chicken.

3 BRING 250ml/9fl oz/1 cup water to the boil and pour this into the pan.

4 STIR the ginger and green peppers into the pan and then simmer, uncovered, for 5 minutes, stirring occasionally, until the sauce thickens and the chicken is cooked through. Check by cutting a piece of chicken in half – the juices should run clear. Serve hot with Naans (see page 26).

CREAMY CHICKEN CURRY

KASHMIRI KORMA

SERVES 4   PREPARATION TIME: 10 MINUTES
COOKING TIME: 20–25 MINUTES

Korma *just means a mild curry. Yet, it is actually a very rich stew in which the meat, chicken or vegetables and nuts are braised in cream, yogurt or coconut milk.*

4 tbsp **vegetable oil**

3 **garlic** cloves

2 **onions**, finely chopped

2 **green chillies**, finely chopped

1 tsp **ground cumin**

1 tsp **ground coriander**

½ tsp **turmeric**

¼ tsp **salt**

4 **green cardamom pods**, slightly crushed

2 tsp **tomato purée**

500g/1lb 2oz boneless, skinless **chicken breasts**, cut into bite-sized pieces

250ml/9fl oz/1 cup **coconut milk**

20 **cashew nuts**, ground

5cm/2in piece **root ginger**, peeled and grated

a generous pinch **Garam Masala** (*see page 23*)

1 **HEAT** the oil in a large saucepan or wok over a medium heat and add the garlic, onions and chillies. Cook, stirring frequently, for 6–8 minutes until the onions turn golden brown.

2 **STIR** in the cumin, coriander, turmeric, salt and cardamom pods and fry for 1 minute, then stir in the tomato purée.

3 **ADD** the chicken pieces, reduce the heat to low and fry, stirring, for 7–8 minutes, or until they change colour. Bring 250ml/9fl oz/1 cup water to the boil.

4 **ADD** the water and the coconut milk to the chicken, then add the ground nuts. Simmer, uncovered, stirring occasionally, for 7 minutes, or until the chicken is cooked through. Check by cutting a piece of chicken in half – the juices should run clear.

5 **STIR** in the ginger and sprinkle over the garam masala. Serve hot.

HYDERABADI-STYLE LAMB

HYDERABADI GOSHT

SERVES 4   PREPARATION TIME: 15 MINUTES
COOKING TIME: 1 HOUR 15 MINUTES

Hyderabad, the capital city of Andhra Pradesh, has a strong fusion of Islamic culture and southern Indian traditions, which are reflected in its cuisine.

85g/3oz **butter** or **ghee**

5cm/2in piece **root ginger**, peeled and chopped

2 **onions**, sliced

7 **black peppercorns**

7 **garlic** cloves, chopped

5 **cloves**

4 **green cardamom pods**

3 **dried red chillies**, chopped in half

2 **cinnamon sticks**

500g/1lb 2oz boneless **stewing lamb**, chopped

375ml/13fl oz/1½ cups **natural yogurt**, whisked

16 **cashew nuts**, ground

1 tsp **turmeric**

1 tsp **cornflour**

½ tsp **salt**

1 MELT the butter or ghee in a flameproof casserole with a tight-fitting lid over a medium heat. Add the ginger, onions, peppercorns, garlic, cloves, cardamom pods, chillies and cinnamon sticks and fry, stirring frequently, for 5 minutes until the onions start to soften and you can smell the aroma of the spices. Watch carefully so the spices do not burn.

2 TIP in the lamb and continue frying, stirring, for 10 minutes, or until it looks brown. Bring 625ml/21½fl oz/2½ cups water to the boil while the lamb is cooking.

3 POUR the boiling water into the pan and return to the boil, stirring once or twice. Cover the pan, reduce the heat to low and simmer for 55 minutes–1 hour until the meat is tender.

4 MIX the yogurt, cashew nuts, turmeric, cornflour and salt in a bowl. Stir into the lamb mixture and simmer, uncovered, for 3 minutes. Bring 125ml/4fl oz/½ cup water to the boil and stir into the lamb. Simmer for a further 2 minutes, or until droplets of oil appear on the surface. Serve with Pulao Rice with Peas (see page 32) and Mint and Yogurt Chutney (see page 19).

LAMB MEATBALLS *MALAI KOFTA*

MAKES **16** PREPARATION TIME: **20** MINUTES
COOKING TIME: **25** MINUTES

*In their simplest form, koftas are meatballs flavoured with spices.
However, in northern Indian cuisine, they are often cooked in a spicy
aromatic sauce with a rich garnish of nuts and cream.*

500g/1lb 2oz **minced lamb**

5cm/2in piece **root ginger**, peeled and grated

2 **green chillies**, chopped

2 **garlic** cloves, crushed

1 tsp **paprika**

1 tsp **salt**

3 tbsp **vegetable oil**

2 **onions**, finely chopped

½ tsp **ground cumin**

½ tsp **ground coriander**

½ tsp **turmeric**

½ tsp **chilli powder**

½ tsp **Garam Masala** (*see page 23*)

1 tsp **tomato purée**

2 tbsp **double cream**

a handful **sliced almonds**

1 **PUT** the lamb in a large bowl and use your hands to mix in the ginger, chillies, garlic, paprika and ½ teaspoon of the salt. Wet your hands and roll the mixture into 16 meatballs of equal size.

2 **HEAT** 3 tablespoons oil in a large frying pan over a medium-high heat. Add the meatballs and fry for 6–7 minutes, turning them in the oil until they are light brown. It might be necessary to do this in batches, depending on the size of your pan. Add extra oil to the pan, if necessary. Use a slotted spoon to remove the meatballs from the pan and set aside.

3 **TIP** the onions into the oil remaining in the pan and fry, stirring frequently, for 6–8 minutes until they are golden brown. Bring 500ml/ 17fl oz/2 cups water to the boil while the onions are frying.

4 **ADD** the cumin, coriander, turmeric, chilli powder, garam masala and remaining ½ teaspoon salt. Fry, stirring occasionally, for 1 minute until you can smell the aroma of the spices. Stir in the tomato purée.

5 **RETURN** the meatballs to the pan and pour in the boiling water. Reduce the heat to low, cover and leave to simmer for 6–8 minutes until small droplets of oil appear on the surface.

6 **SWIRL** in the cream and sprinkle with the almonds. Serve hot with Naans (see page 26).

ROGAN JOSH *MUTTON MASALEDAAR*

SERVES 4   PREPARATION TIME: 20 MINUTES
COOKING TIME: 1 HOUR

*From Kashmir in northern India, this is another restaurant favourite
that is quite easy to cook at home.*

3 tbsp **vegetable oil**

2.5cm/1in piece **cinnamon stick**
   or **cassia bark**

3 **green cardamom pods**

2 **bay leaves**

2 **onions**, finely chopped

2 **garlic** cloves, finely chopped

1 tbsp **butter** or **ghee**

¼ tsp **turmeric**

¼ tsp **chilli powder**

½ tsp **ground cumin**

½ tsp **ground coriander**

1 tsp **tomato purée**

500g/1lb 2oz boneless **stewing lamb**, chopped

¼ tsp **salt**

a pinch **Garam Masala** (*see page 23*)

1 tsp freshly squeezed **lemon juice**

1 HEAT the oil in a large flameproof casserole over a medium heat.
   Add the cinnamon or cassia bark, the cardamom pods and bay leaves
   and fry, stirring, for 30 seconds, or until the spices splutter and you can
   smell their aroma. Watch them carefully so they do not burn.

2 ADD the onions, garlic and butter or ghee and fry, stirring occasionally,
   for 8–10 minutes until the onions are caramelized.

3 STIR in the turmeric, chilli powder, cumin and coriander and stir
   for about 30 seconds. Stir in the tomato purée.

4 TIP in the lamb and fry for 5–7 minutes until it looks brown.

5 BRING 375ml/13fl oz/1½ cups water to the boil while the lamb
   is frying. Pour the boiling water over the lamb. Return to the boil,
   then cover the pan, reduce the heat and simmer for 40 minutes,
   or until the meat is tender and droplets of oil appear on the surface.

6 UNCOVER the casserole, add the salt and sprinkle over the garam
   masala, then stir in the lemon juice. Serve hot.

LUCKNOWI-STYLE LAMB BIRYANI

LUCKNOWI BIRYANI

SERVES 4   PREPARATION TIME: 10 MINUTES, PLUS COOKING THE RICE
COOKING TIME: 1 HOUR 30 MINUTES

Biryanis are always cooked with basmati rice from India or Pakistan, which retains its shape when cooked. A meal in itself, this dish takes a little more time and practice than most, but it is worth the effort.

6 tbsp **butter** or **ghee**

250ml/9fl oz/1 cup **natural yogurt**, whisked

5cm/2in piece **root ginger**, peeled and grated

½ tsp **salt**

¼ tsp **chilli powder**

500g/1lb 2oz boneless **stewing lamb**, chopped

15–20 **saffron strands**, soaked in 2 tbsp **milk**

1 tsp **Garam Masala** (*see page 23*)

1 recipe quantity **Plain Basmati Rice**
   (*see page 31*), cooked

1 MELT 4 tablespoons of the butter or ghee in a large saucepan with a tight-fitting lid over a medium heat. Stir in the yogurt, ginger, salt and chilli powder. Tip in the lamb and cook, stirring frequently, for 5 minutes.

2 BRING 500ml/17fl oz/2 cups water to the boil while the lamb is cooking. Pour the boiling water into the pan, cover and simmer for 45–50 minutes until the meat is tender.

3 STIR the saffron-flavoured milk and garam masala into the lamb.

4 SIMMER the lamb, uncovered, for a further 5–7 minutes until most of the water has evaporated and you are left with a runny gravy.

5 PREHEAT the oven to 180°C/350°F/Gas 4 and grease the base of a large flameproof casserole with 1 tablespoon of the butter or ghee.

6 PUT half of the meat in the casserole. Cover with half the cooked rice, then layer with the remaining lamb and rice. Dot the remaining 1 tablespoon butter or ghee over the top.

7 COVER the casserole and bake in the oven for 20–25 minutes until all the ingredients are hot. Serve immediately.

MINCED LAMB WITH CUMIN AND GINGER *KEEMA MASALA*

SERVES **4** PREPARATION TIME: **10** MINUTES
COOKING TIME: **20** MINUTES

This recipe can also be used as a filling for meat samosas. Simply use the pastry recipe on page 30 and follow the assembly and frying instructions in the recipe for Vegetable Samosas on page 36.

3 tbsp **groundnut oil**

4 **garlic** cloves, chopped

2 **onions**, chopped

2 **green chillies**, chopped

1 tsp **ground cumin**

1 tsp **ground coriander**

¼ tsp **turmeric**

¼ tsp **salt**

2 tsp **tomato purée**

500g/1lb 2oz **minced lamb**

5cm/2in piece **root ginger**, peeled and grated

¼ tsp **Garam Masala** *(see page 23)*

a few **coriander leaves**

1 **HEAT** the oil in a large saucepan or wok over a medium heat. Add the garlic, onions and chillies and fry, stirring frequently, for 6–8 minutes until the onions turn golden brown.

2 **STIR** in the cumin, ground coriander, turmeric, salt and tomato purée, then reduce the heat and continue frying for a further 1 minute.

3 **TIP** in the lamb, increase the heat and continue frying, stirring, for 8–10 minutes, using a wooden spoon to break up the mince, until it is no longer pink.

4 **ADD** the ginger and garam masala, stir well, then sprinkle with the coriander leaves. Serve hot with Chapatis (see page 29) and Cucumber Relish (see page 22).

ROAST LAMB WITH WARMING SPICES

RAAN MASALEDAAR

SERVES 4 PREPARATION TIME: 10 MINUTES, PLUS AT LEAST 1 HOUR
MARINATING TIME COOKING TIME: 2 HOURS

This dish of yogurt-marinated and roasted leg of lamb comes from the border of northern India and Pakistan. It is a common delicacy in North-West Frontier cuisine, where mutton is often used instead of lamb.

1.5kg/3lb 5oz **leg of lamb** on the bone

5cm/2in piece **root ginger**, peeled and grated

1 **onion**, finely chopped

4 tbsp **natural yogurt**, whisked

4 tbsp **vegetable oil**

1 tsp **Garam Masala** (*see page 23*)

½ tsp **chilli powder**

½ tsp **salt**

1 PRICK the flesh of the lamb all over with a skewer or sharp knife.

2 PUT the ginger, onion, yogurt, oil, garam masala, chilli powder and salt in a large bowl and mix well.

3 ADD the lamb to the bowl and use your hands to smear the marinade all over the lamb, then cover and place in the fridge for at least 1 hour, or overnight if time allows. Remove the lamb from the fridge 20 minutes before cooking.

4 PREHEAT the oven to 180°C/350°F/Gas 4.

5 PUT the lamb in a roasting tin, cover with foil and roast for 2 hours. Baste with the juices in the tin after 1 hour, then continue roasting for the remaining 1 hour, or until the flesh is tender when you pierce it with a fork.

6 REMOVE the lamb from the oven and leave to rest, still covered with the foil, for about 15 minutes before carving and serving.

SPICED LAMB CHOPS *KARAHI LAMB*

**SERVES 4   PREPARATION TIME: 15 MINUTES
COOKING TIME: 25 MINUTES**

Karahi is a style of cooking that comes from Kashmir in northern India, where the curries are cooked in a cast-iron pan with a rounded base and two handles, also called a karahi. *A wok or large frying pan with a cover makes an ideal substitute for preparing this particularly comforting recipe.*

---

3 tbsp **vegetable oil**

4 **lamb loin chops** (about 150g/5½oz each)

4 **garlic** cloves, finely chopped

2 **green chillies**, finely chopped

1 **onion**, finely chopped

4 **green cardamom pods**

1 tsp **ground cumin**

1 tsp **ground coriander**

¼ tsp **turmeric**

¼ tsp **ground cinnamon**

¼ tsp **salt**

2 tbsp **tomato purée**

¼ tsp **Garam Masala** (*see page 23*)

5cm/2in piece **root ginger**, peeled and grated

1 **HEAT** the oil in a wok or large frying pan with a tight-fitting lid over a medium heat. Add the lamb chops, garlic, chillies, onion and cardamom pods and fry, stirring, for 12 minutes, or until the lamb changes colour. Bring 310ml/10¾fl oz/1¼ cups water to the boil.

2 **STIR** the cumin, coriander, turmeric, cinnamon and salt into the lamb and continue frying for a further 1 minute. Add the tomato purée, then pour in the boiling water.

3 **COVER** the pan, reduce the heat to low and simmer for 12 minutes, or until droplets of oil appear on the surface. Sprinkle with the garam masala and ginger and serve hot with Naans (see page 26).

LAMB WITH PEAS AND RICE

KEEMA MATTAR CHAWAL

SERVES 4 PREPARATION TIME: 15 MINUTES, PLUS COOKING THE RICE
COOKING TIME: 15 MINUTES

1 tbsp **tomato purée**

4 tbsp **vegetable oil**

½ tsp **ground cumin**

½ tsp **ground coriander**

¼ tsp **turmeric**

¼ tsp **chilli powder**

¼ tsp **Garam Masala** (*see page 23*)

¼ tsp **salt**

2 **garlic** cloves, chopped

1 **onion**, chopped

400g/14oz **minced lamb**

150g/5½oz/1 cup shelled **peas**, defrosted
   if frozen

2.5cm/1in piece **root ginger**, peeled and grated

1 recipe quantity **Plain Basmati Rice**
   (*see page 31*), cooked

a few **coriander leaves**

4 tbsp **natural yogurt**

1 MIX the tomato purée with 1 tablespoon of the oil, the cumin, ground coriander, turmeric, chilli powder, garam masala and salt in a small bowl to form a thick paste. Set aside.

2 HEAT the remaining 3 tablespoons oil in a large saucepan or wok over a medium heat. Add the garlic and onion and fry, stirring, for 1 minute.

3 TIP in the minced lamb, increase the heat and continue frying for 8–10 minutes, using a wooden spoon to break up the mince, until it is no longer pink.

4 ADD the spice paste to the lamb and cook, stirring, for 1½ minutes. Stir in the peas and ginger, then add the cooked rice and continue to cook, stirring, until the rice is hot. Sprinkle with coriander leaves and top with a dollop of yogurt. Serve hot with extra yogurt.

GOAN PORK MEATBALLS IN SPICY CURRY

BOLINHAS DE CARNE

MAKES **16** PREPARATION TIME: **15** MINUTES
COOKING TIME: **30–35** MINUTES

5cm/2in piece **root ginger**, peeled and chopped

4 **garlic** cloves

2 **green chillies**, roughly chopped

½ tsp freshly ground **black pepper**

2 ½ tbsp freshly squeezed **lemon juice**

½ tsp **salt**

500g/1lb 2oz **minced pork**

2 tbsp **rice flour**

about 5 tbsp **groundnut oil**

3 **tomatoes**, coarsely chopped

1 **onion**, chopped

½ tsp **paprika**

½ tsp **ground cumin**

½ tsp **ground coriander**

¼ tsp **chilli powder**

½ tsp **Garam Masala** (*see page 23*)

1 PUT the ginger, garlic, chillies, black pepper, 2 tablespoons of the lemon juice and ¼ teaspoon of the salt in a blender and blend until a thick, paste forms. Transfer the paste to a large bowl, add the pork and mix well. Wet your hands and shape the mixture into 16 meatballs of equal size.

2 ROLL the meatballs in the rice flour so they are coated all over.

3 HEAT 2 tablespoons of the oil in a large frying pan over a medium-high heat. Add the meatballs and fry for 3 minutes, turning them in the oil until they are light brown. Work in batches, adding extra oil, if necessary. Remove the meatballs, wipe out the pan and set aside.

4 PUT the tomatoes in the blender and blend until smooth. Set aside.

5 HEAT 3 tablespoons oil in the pan over a medium heat. Add the onion and fry, stirring occasionally, for 6–8 minutes until golden brown. Stir ½ tablespoon lemon juice, the paprika, cumin, coriander, chilli powder and the remaining ¼ teaspoon salt into the onions and fry for 30 seconds, or until you can smell the aroma of the spices. Bring 250ml/ 9fl oz/1 cup water to the boil while the mixture cooks.

6 ADD the tomatoes to the pan and mix well. Add the meatballs and stir in the boiling water. Bring to the boil, then reduce the heat and simmer, uncovered, for 8–10 minutes until the meatballs are cooked. Sprinkle over the garam masala and serve with Plain Basmati Rice (see page 31).

PORK VINDALOO *VINDALHO DE PORCO*

SERVES 4 PREPARATION TIME: 15 MINUTES, PLUS AT LEAST
2 HOURS MARINATING TIME COOKING TIME: 45 MINUTES

Goanese cuisine is influenced by the region's large Christian communities that eat beef and pork, which are taboo in most other parts of the country.

10 black peppercorns

6 cloves

4 green cardamom pods

1 tsp cumin seeds

1 tsp brown mustard seeds

5cm/2in piece root ginger, peeled and chopped

6 garlic cloves

1 onion, roughly chopped

1 dried red chilli, chopped

½ tsp turmeric

½ tsp ground cinnamon

¼ tsp chilli powder

2 tbsp malt vinegar

1 tsp tomato purée

500g/1lb 2oz boneless leg of pork, cut into bite-sized pieces

3 tbsp groundnut oil

1 HEAT a dry frying pan over a medium-low heat until you can feel the heat rising. Add the peppercorns, cloves, cardamom pods, cumin and mustard seeds and roast, shaking the pan occasionally, until you can smell the aroma of the spices. Watch carefully so they do not burn. Immediately tip the spices on to a plate and leave to cool completely.

2 TRANSFER the spices to a blender along with the ginger, garlic, onion, dried chilli, turmeric, cinnamon, chilli powder, vinegar and tomato purée and blend until a coarse, thick paste forms.

3 PLACE the pork in a large, non-metallic bowl, add the paste and use your hands to rub it into the meat. Cover the bowl with cling film and refrigerate for at least 2 hours or overnight. Remove from the fridge about 15 minutes before cooking.

4 HEAT the oil in a large saucepan with a tight-fitting lid. Add the pork and fry for 10 minutes, or until all the pieces are light brown. Bring 375ml/13fl oz/1½ cups water to the boil while the pork is cooking.

5 POUR the boiling water into the pan and return to the boil. Reduce the heat, cover and simmer for 25–30 minutes until the pork is tender. Serve hot with Plain Basmati Rice (see page 31) and Mango Chutney (see page 19).

GOAN FISH CURRY *AMBOTIK*

SERVES 4   PREPARATION TIME: **15** MINUTES
COOKING TIME: **15–20** MINUTES

½ tsp **salt**

450g/1lb skinless **lemon sole** or **hoki** fillets, cut into 6cm/2½in pieces

1 tsp **tamarind pulp**

50g/1¾oz **creamed coconut**, crumbled

2.5cm/1in piece **root ginger**, peeled and chopped

5 **garlic** cloves

1 tsp **sugar**

1 **dried red chilli**, roughly chopped

¼ tsp **chilli powder**

¼ tsp **turmeric**

¼ tsp **ground cumin**

¼ tsp **ground coriander**

¼ tsp freshly ground **black pepper**

¼ tsp **ground cinnamon**

3 tbsp **groundnut oil**

1 **onion**, finely chopped

1 **tomato**, chopped

1 SPRINKLE the salt over the fish and set aside.

2 PUT the tamarind pulp in a small heatproof bowl, pour over enough boiling water to cover and leave to stand for 10 minutes. Use a wooden spoon to press the pulp and release the seeds and fibres, then strain through a nylon sieve into a bowl, pressing with the back of the spoon to extract as much juice as possible. Discard the pulp and set aside the juice.

3 TRANSFER the tamarind juice to a blender. Add the creamed coconut, ginger, garlic, sugar, dried chilli, chilli powder, turmeric, cumin, coriander, black pepper, cinnamon, 1 tablespoon of the oil and 1 tablespoon water and blend until the mixture forms a thick, coarse paste.

4 HEAT the remaining 2 tablespoons oil in a large saucepan or wok over a medium heat. Add the onion and fry, stirring constantly, for 6–8 minutes until golden brown. Add the tomato and continue frying, stirring, for 2–3 minutes until it is soft. Bring 310ml/10¾fl oz/1¼ cups water to the boil while the tomato is cooking.

5 TIP in the tamarind paste with the boiling water and return to the boil. Reduce the heat and simmer, uncovered, for 2 minutes. Add the fish to the pan and simmer for a further 5–6 minutes, taking care not to break up the pieces, until it is cooked through and the flesh flakes easily. Serve hot.

HALIBUT WITH GREEN CHILLIES AND CORIANDER

POTHAL CURRY

SERVES 4   PREPARATION TIME: 10 MINUTES
COOKING TIME: 15 MINUTES

½ tsp **turmeric**

¼ tsp **salt**

a pinch **chilli powder**

4 boneless **halibut** fillets (about 100g/3½oz each), skinned

2 tbsp **tamarind pulp**

a handful **coriander leaves**

5cm/2in piece **root ginger**, peeled and chopped

4 **garlic** cloves

2 **green chillies**, chopped

1 tsp **ground cumin**

2 tbsp **groundnut oil**

1 SPRINKLE the turmeric, salt and chilli powder over the halibut and set aside.

2 PUT the tamarind pulp in a small heatproof bowl, pour over enough boiling water to cover and leave to stand for 10 minutes. Use a wooden spoon to press the pulp and release the seeds and fibres, then strain through a nylon sieve into a bowl, pressing with the back of the spoon to extract as much juice as possible. Discard the pulp, stir 4 tablespoons water into the tamarind juice and set aside.

3 SET a few coriander leaves aside. Chop the remaining ones and put them in a blender with the ginger, garlic, chillies, cumin and 125ml/4fl oz/½ cup water. Blend until the mixture forms a coarse watery paste.

4 HEAT the oil in a large frying pan over a medium heat. Add the fish and fry for 3–4 minutes, turning once, until lightly browned on both sides. Remove from the pan and set aside.

5 ADD the coriander paste to the oil remaining in the pan and simmer for about 3 minutes, stirring occasionally, until droplets of oil appear on the surface. Return the fish to the pan and simmer for 1 minute.

6 POUR the tamarind juice into the pan. Simmer for a further 1 minute, then serve with the remaining coriander leaves.

WHITE FISH IN TOMATO CURRY

TAMATAR MACHCHI

**SERVES 4   PREPARATION TIME: 10 MINUTES
COOKING TIME: 20 MINUTES**

Using only a few basic spices brings out the subtle and delicate flavours of the fish in this quick and zesty dish. The white fish can also be replaced with an oily fish, such as tuna or mackerel.

½ tsp **turmeric**

¼ tsp **salt**

500g/1lb 2oz skinless, boneless **sole, coley** or **cod** fillets, cut into 7.5cm/3in pieces

3 tbsp **vegetable oil**

5cm/2in piece **root ginger**, peeled and chopped

6 **garlic** cloves, chopped

2 **onions**, finely chopped

2 large **plum tomatoes**, finely chopped

½ tsp **ground cumin**

½ tsp **ground coriander**

¼ tsp **chilli powder**

1 SPRINKLE the turmeric and salt over the fish and set aside.

2 HEAT the oil in a large saucepan over a medium heat. Add the ginger, garlic and onions and fry, stirring frequently, for 6–8 minutes until the onions are golden brown.

3 TIP in the tomatoes, cumin, coriander and chilli powder and cook, stirring, for 2 minutes. Bring 185ml/6fl oz/¾ cup water to the boil.

4 PUT the fish in the pan and simmer for a further 2 minutes, taking care not to break up the pieces.

5 POUR over the boiling water and simmer for a further 8–9 minutes until the fish is cooked through and the flesh flakes easily. Serve hot with Potatoes with Cauliflower (see page 72) and Chapatis (see page 29).

SPICED WHITE FISH COOKED IN COCONUT

MEEN MOLEE

SERVES 4 PREPARATION TIME: 10 MINUTES
COOKING TIME: 15 MINUTES

The combination of the coconut and tamarind gives this dish a distinctive sweet-and-sour flavour that is typical of Kerala, in the south of India.

2 tbsp **tamarind pulp**

1 tsp **ground cumin**

1 tsp **ground coriander**

a pinch **chilli powder**

¼ tsp **turmeric**

¼ tsp **salt**

300g/10½oz **lemon sole** fillets, skinned, trimmed and cut into 7.5cm/3in pieces

2 tbsp **vegetable oil**

4 **garlic** cloves, chopped

55g/1¾oz **creamed coconut**, crumbled

1 PUT the tamarind pulp in a small heatproof bowl, pour over enough boiling water to cover and leave to stand for 10 minutes. Use a wooden spoon to press the pulp and release the seeds and fibres, then strain through a nylon sieve into a bowl, pressing with the back of the spoon to extract as much juice as possible. Discard the pulp. Bring 250ml/9fl oz/1 cup water to the boil.

2 SPRINKLE the turmeric and salt over the fish. Stir the cumin, coriander, chilli powder and boiling water into the tamarind juice, then set aside.

3 HEAT the oil in a large frying pan over a medium heat. Add the fish and fry for 3–4 minutes, turning occasionally and taking care not to break up the pieces. Remove the fish from the pan and set aside.

4 REDUCE the heat, add the garlic to the oil remaining in the pan and fry, stirring, for 30 seconds, or until golden. Watch so it does not burn.

5 RETURN the fish to the pan. Stir in the creamed coconut, tamarind liquid and 4 tablespoons boiling water. Simmer for a further 3–4 minutes until the flavours blend and the fish is cooked through and flakes easily. Serve hot with Plain Basmati Rice (see page 31).

TANDOORI-STYLE TROUT

TANDOORI MACHCHI

SERVES 4 PREPARATION TIME: 10 MINUTES, PLUS 30 MINUTES
MARINATING TIME COOKING TIME: 15 MINUTES

Like all tandoori dishes, this tender, flaky trout dish can also be cooked on a barbecue – turning an outdoor summer meal into a truly special occasion.

4 whole **trout**, gutted

5cm/2in piece **root ginger**, peeled and coarsely chopped

6 **garlic** cloves

3 tbsp **vegetable oil**

1 tbsp freshly squeezed **lemon juice**

2 tsp **tomato purée**

1 tsp **paprika**

½ tsp **chilli powder**

½ tsp **ground cumin**

½ tsp **salt**

¼ tsp **turmeric**

a few **coriander leaves**

1 CUT 4 diagonal slits in each trout, 2 on either side. Place the fish on a deep, non-metallic dish large enough to hold them in a single layer.

2 PUT all the remaining ingredients except the coriander leaves in a blender and blend until a coarse paste forms.

3 POUR the paste over the trout and rub it into the flesh and the slits. Cover the dish with cling film and place it in the fridge for 30 minutes to allow the marinade to soak into the fish.

4 PREHEAT the grill to medium. Place the fish on a foil-lined grill pan tray and grill for 7–8 minutes on each side until the skin blisters and the fish is white and flaky inside when you cut along the backbone. Serve with the coriander leaves, Tomato, Onion and Chilli Salad (see page 160) and Coriander Chutney (see page 19).

TUNA WITH PICKLING SPICES

MAACHER JHOL

SERVES 4 PREPARATION TIME: **10** MINUTES
COOKING TIME: **25–30** MINUTES

The aromatic spice blend panch phoron features many of the spices used to make Indian pickles. Here, it lends a distinct pungent flavour to seared tuna steaks.

1 tsp **salt**

1 tsp **turmeric**

4 **tuna steaks**

5 tbsp **groundnut oil**

1 tsp **Panch Phoron** (*see page 24*)

400g/14oz **potatoes**, peeled and quartered

5cm/2in piece **root ginger**, peeled

6 **garlic** cloves

4 **green chillies**

a pinch **chilli powder**

a few **coriander leaves**

1 SPRINKLE the salt and turmeric over the tuna. Heat 4 tablespoons of the oil in a large frying pan over a medium heat. Add the tuna steaks and lightly fry on each side for 3 minutes, or until they are seared. Remove them from the pan and set aside.

2 ADD the remaining 1 tablespoon oil to the pan, tip in the panch phoron and fry for about 30 seconds, stirring constantly, or until you can smell the aroma. Watch carefully so the mixture does not burn.

3 ADD the potatoes and fry for about 5 minutes, stirring occasionally. Bring 500ml/17fl oz/2 cups water to the boil.

4 PUT the ginger, garlic, chillies and chilli powder in a blender and blend until a coarse paste forms. Tip the paste into the pan and continue frying for a further 2 minutes.

5 STIR in the boiling water and return to the boil. Reduce the heat and simmer for a further 6–7 minutes until the potatoes are tender.

6 RETURN the tuna to the pan and simmer for a further 4 minutes, or until the fish is cooked to your liking. Serve hot, sprinkled with the coriander leaves.

MALABAR KING PRAWN CURRY

CHEMMEEN CURRY

SERVES 4 PREPARATION TIME: 10 MINUTES
COOKING TIME: 15–20 MINUTES

*Velvety coconut milk and succulent seafood, the signature elements
of Malabar cuisine, combine here in a mouthwatering curry.*

½ tsp **turmeric**

½ tsp **salt**

20 raw **king prawns**, peeled and black veins
removed (*see page 18*)

4 tbsp **groundnut oil**

5cm/2in piece **root ginger**, peeled and grated

8 **shallots**, chopped

6 **garlic** cloves, chopped

2 **green chillies**, chopped

2 **tomatoes**, chopped

a pinch **chilli powder** (optional)

310ml/10¾fl oz/1¼ cups **coconut milk**

8 **curry leaves**

½ tsp **brown mustard seeds**

1 SPRINKLE the turmeric and salt over the prawns and set aside.

2 HEAT 3 tablespoons of the oil in a large frying pan over a medium
heat. Add the ginger, shallots, garlic and green chillies and fry, stirring
occasionally, for 6–8 minutes until the shallots are golden brown.
Bring 125ml/4fl oz/½ cup water to the boil.

3 ADD the tomatoes and chilli powder, if using, and fry for a further
2 minutes. Tip in the prawns and continue stirring for 2 minutes.

4 POUR the coconut milk into the pan with the boiling water and
simmer for 2 minutes, or just until the prawns turn opaque.

5 HEAT the remaining 1 tablespoon oil in a small frying pan over
a medium heat. Add the curry leaves and mustard seeds and fry for
30 seconds, or until the seeds splutter. Watch carefully so the leaves
and seeds do not burn. Stir them into the prawn curry. Serve hot.

PRAWNS WITH GARLIC AND CHILLI

JHINGA PATIA

SERVES 4 PREPARATION TIME: 20 MINUTES
COOKING TIME: 12 MINUTES

*Piquant tomato purée adds a level of flavour to these spicy
and succulent prawns.*

4 tbsp **groundnut oil**

1 **onion**, chopped

6 **garlic** cloves, crushed

½ tsp **ground cumin**

½ tsp **salt**

¼ tsp **turmeric**

¼ tsp **ground coriander**

¼ tsp **chilli powder**

1 tbsp **tomato purée**

400g/14oz raw **king prawns**, peeled and black
  veins removed (*see page 18*)

¼ tsp **Garam Masala** (*see page 23*)

a few **coriander leaves**, chopped

1 **HEAT** the oil in a large frying pan over a medium heat. Add the onion and fry, stirring frequently, for 6–8 minutes until golden brown. Bring 125ml/4fl oz/½ cup water to the boil.

2 **ADD** the garlic, cumin, salt, turmeric, ground coriander, chilli powder and tomato purée to the onion and continue frying, stirring constantly, for 1 minute. Tip in the prawns and fry, stirring, for 2–3 minutes.

3 **POUR** over the boiling water and fry for a further 1 minute, or just until the prawns turn opaque and curl.

4 **SPRINKLE** the garam masala and coriander leaves over the dish. Serve hot with Spiced Rice (see page 32).

PRAWNS WITH HOT-AND-SOUR CURRY

KOLAMBICHE KAALVAN

SERVES **4**   PREPARATION TIME: **10** MINUTES
COOKING TIME: **5–6** MINUTES

*A kaalvan is a thin gravy-based dish made with meat, poultry or seafood.
A traditional recipe from the western state of Maharashtra, it can also
be made with fish, such as pomfret or cod.*

2 tbsp **tamarind pulp**

1 tsp **ground cumin**

1 tsp **ground coriander**

1 tsp **rice flour**

½ tsp **chilli powder**

½ tsp **turmeric**

¼ tsp **salt**

400g/14oz raw **king prawns**, peeled
and black veins removed (*see page 18*)

2 tbsp **groundnut oil**

4 **garlic** cloves, slightly crushed

a few **coriander leaves**

1 **PUT** the tamarind pulp in a small heatproof bowl, pour over enough boiling water to cover and leave to stand for 10 minutes. Use a wooden spoon to press the pulp and release the seeds and fibres, then strain through a nylon sieve into a bowl, pressing with the back of the spoon to extract as much juice as possible. Discard the pulp.

2 **ADD** the cumin, ground coriander, rice flour, chilli powder and turmeric to the tamarind juice and stir to make a lumpy paste.

3 **BRING** 375ml/13fl oz/1½ cups water to the boil. Sprinkle the salt over the prawns. Heat the oil in a large wok or frying pan over a medium heat. Add the prawns and garlic and fry, stirring constantly, for 1 minute. Stir in the tamarind paste and continue frying, stirring, for a further 1 minute.

4 **POUR** over the boiling water and simmer for a further 3 minutes, stirring occasionally, or just until the prawns turn opaque and curl. Scatter with coriander leaves and serve.

BALTI POTATOES *HARYALI ALOO*

SERVES 4 PREPARATION TIME: 15 MINUTES
COOKING TIME: 30–35 MINUTES

Balti *means bucket and is the name given to a style of cuisine that in all probability was developed in Birmingham, England. Balti-style dishes are named after the pot or vessel in which they are cooked and served, although a wok works just as well for cooking in. This dish is a lovely accompaniment to lamb.*

1 kg/2lb 4oz **waxy potatoes**, peeled and cut into 5cm/2in pieces

4 tbsp **vegetable oil**

2 **onions**, finely chopped

1 bunch **coriander leaves**

a few **mint leaves**

5cm/2in piece **root ginger**, peeled and coarsely chopped

4 **garlic** cloves

3 **green chillies**, chopped

½ tsp **salt**

¼ tsp **turmeric**

1 BRING a large saucepan of water to the boil over a high heat. Tip in the potatoes, return the water to the boil and continue boiling for 10 minutes, or until the potatoes are almost tender. Drain and set aside.

2 HEAT the oil in a wok over a medium heat. Add the onions and fry, stirring frequently, for 6–8 minutes until they are golden brown.

3 PUT the coriander, mint, ginger, garlic and chillies in a blender and blend until the mixture forms a coarse paste. Bring 375ml/13fl oz/ 1½ cups water to the boil.

4 STIR the salt and turmeric to the onions and cook for 1 minute, then add the coriander paste. Continue frying, stirring constantly, for 3–4 minutes. Tip in the potatoes and continue frying, stirring, for a further 3 minutes.

5 POUR the boiling water over the potatoes and return to the boil. Reduce the heat and simmer, uncovered, for 6–7 minutes until they are tender, then serve.

MAHARASHTRIAN LENTILS *VARAN*

SERVES 4   PREPARATION TIME: 5 MINUTES
COOKING TIME: 30 MINUTES

The cuisine of Maharashtra, in western India, varies from extremely mild in flavour to alarmingly hot. This simple yet flavoursome dal, or lentil stew, seasoned only with turmeric and asafoetida, is a comforting dish that perfectly complements fiery hot curries.

250g/9oz/1 cup **split yellow lentils**

½ tsp **turmeric**

50g/1¾oz **butter** or **ghee**

1 tsp **sugar**

½ tsp **salt**

a pinch **asafoetida**

a few **coriander leaves**

1 PUT 625ml/21½fl oz/2½ cups water in a large saucepan and bring to the boil over a high heat. Add the lentils and turmeric to the pan and return to the boil. Partially cover the pan, reduce the heat to low and leave the lentils to simmer, stirring occasionally, for 25 minutes, or until they are mushy. Watch carefully so the lentils do not burn. Top up with extra boiling water, if necessary.

2 MELT the butter or ghee in another pan over a medium heat, then stir in the sugar, salt and asafoetida. Add this mixture to the lentils. Bring 310ml/10¾fl oz/1¼ cups water to the boil and stir into the lentils.

3 MASH the lentils a little against the side of the pan and simmer for a further 3 minutes. Serve hot with the coriander leaves.

TEMPERED RED LENTILS

TARKA DAL

SERVES 4   PREPARATION TIME: 10 MINUTES
COOKING TIME: 30 MINUTES

Lentils are prepared almost daily in many Indian homes. This recipe produces a rich velvety purée laced with spiced butter, simply made by boiling the pulses, then mashing them and pouring spicy butter over the top. This technique is called tempering.

200g/7oz/generous ¾ cup **split red lentils**

45g/1½oz **butter** or **ghee**

6 **curry leaves**

1 **green chilli**, chopped

½ tsp **brown mustard seeds**

½ tsp **turmeric**

¼ tsp **salt**

a pinch **asafoetida**

1 BRING 500ml/17fl oz/2 cups water to the boil in a large saucepan over a high heat. Add the lentils and return the water to the boil. Partially cover the pan, reduce the heat to low and simmer, uncovered, stirring occasionally, for 20–30 minutes until the mixture becomes mushy. Watch carefully so the lentils do not burn. Top up with extra boiling water, if necessary.

2 MELT the butter in a frying pan over a medium heat. Add the curry leaves, chilli, mustard seeds, turmeric, salt and asafoetida and fry, stirring constantly, for 30 seconds, or until the spices splutter. Watch carefully so they do not burn.

3 STIR the buttery spice mixture into the lentils, then cook for a further 2 minutes. Serve hot with Okra with Mustard Seeds (see page 158).

SPICED BLACK-EYED BEANS

RAUNGI

SERVES 4   PREPARATION TIME: 10 MINUTES
COOKING TIME: 12 MINUTES

Black-eyed beans, often eaten after prayers in southern India, have a fine, almost nutty flavour. The addition of yogurt, ginger and cumin in this recipe results in a comforting and flavoursome dish that can be enjoyed with any favourite meat or vegetarian main dish.

3 tbsp **vegetable oil**

2 cans (400g/14oz each) **black-eyed beans**, drained and rinsed

½ tsp **turmeric**

a pinch **asafoetida**

1 tsp **ground cumin**

½ tsp **salt**

¼ tsp **chilli powder**

4 tbsp **natural yogurt**, whisked

5cm/2in piece **root ginger**, peeled and grated

a handful **coriander leaves**, chopped

1 **HEAT** the oil in a large saucepan over a medium heat. Add the beans, turmeric and asafoetida and stir for 1 minute, or until you can smell the aroma of the spices.

2 **STIR** the cumin, salt and chilli powder. Bring 185ml/6fl oz/¾ cup water to the boil.

3 **POUR** over the boiling water, add the yogurt and stir well. Cover the pan, reduce the heat and simmer for 6–8 minutes until droplets of oil appear on the surface.

4 **SPRINKLE** with the ginger and coriander leaves, then serve hot with Chapatis (see page 29) and Cucumber Relish (see page 22).

SMOKED AUBERGINE

BAINGAN BHARTA

SERVES 4 PREPARATION TIME: 15–20 MINUTES
COOKING TIME: 15 MINUTES

This earthy, aromatic vegetable dish from North India makes a lovely accompaniment to any main meal.

2 large **aubergines**

3 tbsp **vegetable oil**, plus extra for charring the aubergines (optional)

6 **garlic** cloves, finely chopped

2 **onions**, finely chopped

2 **green chillies**, finely chopped

2 tsp **tomato purée**

1 tsp **ground cumin**

¼ tsp **salt**

2.5cm/1in piece **root ginger**, peeled and grated

a pinch **Garam Masala** (*see page 23*)

a few **coriander leaves**, chopped

1 HOLD an aubergine with a pair of tongs over a flame, turning often, until the skin is charred and blistered all over. Repeat with the other aubergine. Alternatively, preheat the grill to high, halve each aubergine and rub the cut surface with a little oil. Place the aubergines, cut side down, on a grill pan and grill for 8–10 minutes until the skin is charred and blistered all over.

2 LEAVE the aubergines until they are cool enough to handle. Cut each one in half lengthways, if they are still whole, and scoop the flesh into a bowl, then mash or chop it and set aside.

3 HEAT the oil in a wok or large saucepan over a medium heat. Add the garlic, onions and chillies and fry, stirring frequently, for 6–8 minutes until the onions are golden brown.

4 ADD the tomato purée, cumin and salt and fry, stirring, for 2 minutes until the mixture becomes quite thick. Stir in the aubergine and cook, stirring, for 3 minutes until the mixture becomes thick and mushy.

5 SPRINKLE with the ginger and garam masala and continue cooking for about 30 seconds. Serve hot, sprinkled with coriander leaves.

CUMIN-INFUSED PEAS

ZEERAWALI MATTAR

SERVES 4   PREPARATION TIME: 2 MINUTES
COOKING TIME: 5 MINUTES

This quick recipe uses a few basic spices to jazz up fresh peas – and is versatile enough to be served hot, chilled or at room temperature. If you cannot get hold of fresh peas, the frozen ones provide a good alternative once defrosted.

2 tbsp **vegetable oil**

½ tsp **brown mustard seeds**

1 tsp **ground cumin**

½ tsp **ground coriander**

¼ tsp **chilli powder**

¼ tsp **turmeric**

¼ tsp **salt**

300g/10½oz/2 cups shelled **peas**, defrosted if frozen

1 tsp freshly squeezed **lemon juice**

1 HEAT the oil in a large frying pan over a medium heat. Add the mustard seeds and fry, stirring constantly, for 30 seconds, or until they splutter. Watch carefully so they do not burn.

2 STIR in the cumin, coriander, chilli powder, turmeric, salt and peas and continue to fry for a further 2 minutes.

3 SPRINKLE the lemon juice and 2 tablespoons water over the peas. Continue cooking for a further 1 minute, or until the peas are tender. Serve hot, or cool completely, cover and refrigerate until required.

GREEN BEANS WITH GARLIC AND MUSTARD SEEDS

LAHSUNI RAI BEANS

SERVES 4 PREPARATION TIME: 10 MINUTES
COOKING TIME: 8 MINUTES

Mustard seeds are to southern, south-western and eastern India what cumin seeds are to the north. Used to season just about every savoury preparation, they evoke a hot and nutty flavour once they are heated in oil.

3 tbsp **groundnut oil**

½ tsp **brown mustard seeds**

3 **garlic** cloves, chopped

2 **green chillies**, finely chopped

1 **onion**, finely chopped

400g/14oz fine **green beans**, topped and tailed

1 tsp **ground cumin**

¼ tsp **salt**

1 **HEAT** the oil in a large frying pan over a medium heat. Add the mustard seeds and fry, stirring constantly, for 30 seconds, or until they splutter. Watch carefully so they do not burn.

2 **ADD** the garlic, chillies and onion. Continue frying, stirring frequently, for 3 minutes, or until the onions become soft. Add the beans and fry for a further 1 minute.

3 **STIR** in the cumin and salt and continue frying for 2–3 minutes, or until the beans are tender, then serve.

GREEN PEPPERS WITH CUMIN

SHIMLA MIRCH SABZI

SERVES 4   PREPARATION TIME: 5 MINUTES
COOKING TIME: 10 MINUTES

A touch of turmeric and tomato purée adds a warm golden glow to a quick and colourful dish that can be prepared in a matter of minutes.

2 tbsp **vegetable oil**

2 **garlic** cloves, sliced

1 **onion**, sliced

4 **green peppers**, seeded and cut into strips 2.5cm/1in thick

1 **green chilli**, chopped

¼ tsp **turmeric**

1 tsp **ground cumin**

¼ tsp **salt**

1 **tomato**, chopped

1 tsp **tomato purée**

a pinch **Garam Masala** (*see page 23*)

1 HEAT the oil in a large saucepan over a medium heat. Add the garlic and onion and fry, stirring frequently, for 2 minutes, or until the onion starts to soften.

2 TIP in the peppers, chilli, turmeric, cumin and salt. Continue frying for a further 2 minutes, then stir in the chopped tomato and fry for 2 minutes more until the tomato starts to soften.

3 ADD the tomato purée and continue frying, stirring, for a further 2 minutes, or until the peppers are tender.

4 STIR in the garam masala and serve hot with Fried Pulses (see page 64) and Chapatis (see page 29).

CABBAGE WITH RED CHILLIES

PATTA GOBHI KI SABZI

SERVES 4 PREPARATION TIME: 5 MINUTES
COOKING TIME: 7 MINUTES

Indian cooks from the south use coconut as frequently as cooks in the north use onions – and it features in both sweet and savoury dishes. The desiccated coconut in this recipe can be replaced with freshly grated coconut.

3 tbsp **vegetable oil**

2 **dried red chillies**

1 tsp **brown mustard seeds**

400g/14oz **white cabbage**, finely shredded

½ tsp **salt**

1 tsp freshly squeezed **lemon juice**

1 tbsp **desiccated coconut**

1 HEAT the oil in a large frying pan or wok over a medium heat. Add the chillies and mustard seeds and fry for 30 seconds, stirring constantly, or until they begin to splutter. Watch carefully so they do not burn.

2 ADD the cabbage and salt, then increase the heat to medium-high. Fry, stirring constantly, for 5–6 minutes until the cabbage is tender.

3 STIR in the lemon juice and coconut. Serve hot.

SPICED SPRING GREENS

HARI SABZI

SERVES **4**   PREPARATION TIME: **5** MINUTES
COOKING TIME: **11** MINUTES

Indians use a wide variety of leafy greens in their cooking, including radish, carrot, pumpkin and turnip leaves. Kale makes a good substitute for the spring greens in this dish, which is traditionally prepared with potatoes, beans or peas.

2 tbsp **vegetable oil**

2 **garlic** cloves, crushed

1 **green chilli**, chopped

½ tsp **salt**

425g/15oz **spring greens**, well rinsed and chopped

1 HEAT the oil in a large frying pan or wok over a medium-high heat. Add the garlic and fry, stirring, for 30 seconds. Watch carefully so the garlic does not burn.

2 ADD the chilli, salt and spring greens and fry, stirring constantly, for 10 minutes, or until the greens are tender. Serve hot with Tempered Red Lentils (see page 142).

OKRA WITH MUSTARD SEEDS

RAI BHINDI

SERVES 4 PREPARATION TIME: 15 MINUTES
COOKING TIME: 12 MINUTES

Okra, also known as ladies' fingers because of its long, slender shape, is a favourite of many Indian cooks. In this dry dish, the lightly spiced okra remains deliciously crisp and the mustard and cumin impart a subtle nutty flavour. It is essential to dry the okra thoroughly after rinsing to prevent the dish becoming soggy when cooked.

450g/1lb **okra**, well rinsed and thoroughly dried

3 tbsp **vegetable oil**

½ tsp **brown mustard seeds**

1 **green chilli**, finely chopped

½ tsp **ground cumin**

¼ tsp **salt**

1 TRIM off the stalks from the okra and cut the pods into 2.5cm/1in long pieces.

2 HEAT the oil in a large frying pan or wok over a medium heat. Add the mustard seeds and fry, stirring, for 30–40 seconds, or until they splutter. Watch carefully so they do not burn.

3 TIP in all the remaining ingredients and increase the heat to medium-high. Continue frying, stirring constantly, for 10–12 minutes until the okra is tender. Serve hot.

TOMATO, ONION AND CHILLI SALAD

TAMATAR PYAAZ AUR MIRCH KA SALAAD

SERVES 4   PREPARATION TIME: 10 MINUTES, PLUS CHILLING

Indian salads are refreshing complements to elaborate dishes that are loaded with spices and flavours. This sharp, tangy recipe is remarkably simple and pairs well with meat or chicken.

2 **tomatoes**, chopped

1 **red onion**, finely chopped

1 **green chilli**, finely chopped

1 tbsp freshly squeezed **lemon juice**

½ tsp **sugar**

a pinch freshly ground **black pepper**

a pinch **salt**

1 PUT all the ingredients in a non-metallic bowl and toss together.

2 COVER the bowl with cling film and refrigerate until required. Taste and adjust the seasoning, adding more salt and pepper, if necessary, just before serving. Serve chilled.

CARROT SALAD

KOSHIMBIR

SERVES 4   PREPARATION TIME: 10 MINUTES, PLUS CHILLING
COOKING TIME: 3 MINUTES

This Maharashtrian salad, from western India, can also be made with various other vegetables, such as radish or cabbage. More often than not, crushed or ground peanuts are added, as in this recipe, which is a perfect complement to any mild curry.

350g/12oz **carrots**, peeled and coarsely grated

1 **onion**, finely chopped

1 **green chilli**, finely chopped

1 **tomato**, finely chopped

2 tbsp freshly squeezed **lemon juice**

1 tsp **sugar**

½ tsp **salt**

2 tbsp **roasted peanuts**, crushed (optional)

1 tbsp **groundnut oil**

6 **curry leaves**

½ tsp **brown** or **black mustard seeds**

¼ tsp **turmeric**

1 PUT the carrots, onion, chilli, tomato, lemon juice, sugar, salt and peanuts, if using, in a large bowl and mix well. Set aside.

2 HEAT the oil in a frying pan over a medium-high heat. Add the curry leaves and mustard seeds and fry, stirring constantly, for 30 seconds, or until they splutter. Watch carefully so the mixture does not burn.

3 ADD the turmeric, then drizzle the hot mixture over the salad. Stir well.

4 SET ASIDE until the salad cools completely, then cover the bowl with cling film and refrigerate until required. Serve chilled.

SPROUTED MUNG BEAN SALAD

MOONG SALAAD

SERVES 4   PREPARATION TIME: 10 MINUTES, PLUS CHILLING
COOKING TIME: 2 MINUTES

Sprouted beans are easy to digest and are frequently used in dishes from the western and southern parts of India. They impart a crisp, nutty flavour to dishes like this one.

280g/10oz fresh **mung bean sprouts** (*see page 18*)

a pinch **turmeric**

1 **green chilli**, finely chopped

1 **onion**, finely chopped

2 tbsp freshly squeezed **lemon juice**

½ tsp **sugar**

½ tsp **salt**

a large pinch freshly ground **black pepper**

1 TIP the bean sprouts, turmeric and 2 tablespoons water into a saucepan and heat over a medium heat, stirring, for 2 minutes, or until the bean sprouts wilt.

2 MIX the chilli, onion, lemon juice, sugar, salt and pepper together in a large bowl.

3 ADD the cooked bean sprouts to the chilli mixture and then set aside to cool completely. Cover the bowl with cling film and refrigerate until required. Serve chilled.

CHICKPEA PETIT FOURS

BESAN KI LADDOO

MAKES **16** PREPARATION TIME: **5** MINUTES, PLUS COOLING AND SETTING
COOKING TIME: **11** MINUTES

*These small, nutty-tasting treats are served at teatime and often at the end
of a meal in Indian homes. For an even richer taste, add five or six coarsely
chopped almonds with their skins to the mixture after adding the sugar.*

125g/4½oz **unsalted butter**

200g/7oz/1¾ cups plus 2 tbsp **chickpea** or **gram
flour**, sifted

2 tbsp **milk**

100g/7oz/scant ½ cup **caster sugar**

1 **PUT** the butter and chickpea or gram flour in a saucepan over
a medium heat and stir for about 10 minutes, or until the butter melts,
the flour looks like wet sand and you can smell the nutty roasted
aroma. Watch carefully so the mixture does not burn.

2 **STIR** in the milk, then remove the pan from the heat.

3 **TIP** in the sugar and mix thoroughly with a fork for 2–3 minutes until
the mixture becomes thick and clumpy. Transfer it to a plate and set
aside for about 5 minutes, or until it is cool enough to handle.

4 **WET** your hands and shape the mixture into 16 balls of equal size.

5 **LEAVE** the balls to cool completely. Serve at room temperature, with
Spicy Tea (see page 186). These petit fours can also be transferred to an
airtight container and stored at room temperature for up to 10 days,
or refrigerated for up to 2 weeks.

CASHEW NUT DIAMONDS

KAAJU KI BARFI

MAKES 12–14 DIAMONDS   PREPARATION TIME: 10 MINUTES, PLUS
A LITTLE COOLING TIME   COOKING TIME: 4 MINUTES

This fragrant, fudge-like Indian sweet is served during auspicious Hindu festivals.

200g/7oz/1⅓ cups **cashew nuts**

seeds from 2 **green cardamom pods**
  (*see page 14*)

80g/2¾oz/scant ⅔ cup **icing sugar**

1 PUT the cashew nuts in a heatproof bowl and pour over enough boiling water to cover, then set aside and leave to soak for 10 minutes.

2 CRUSH the cardamom seeds to a powder in a pestle and mortar.

3 DRAIN the cashew nuts, put them in a blender and blend until the mixture forms a thick paste. Set aside.

4 PUT the sugar in a saucepan over a medium heat and cook, stirring constantly, for 2 minutes, or until the sugar melts.

5 STIR in the cashew nut paste and ground cardamom seeds. Spoon the mixture onto greaseproof paper and use a wet palette knife or spatula to spread it into a 10cm/4in square, about 1.5cm/¾in thick. Using a sharp knife, cut the square into diamonds and leave to cool. Serve at room temperature, or transfer to an airtight container and refrigerate for up to 2 weeks.

COCONUT TREATS

NARIYAL LADDOO

MAKES 10–12 PREPARATION TIME: 10 MINUTES
COOKING TIME: 4 MINUTES

Made with only two ingredients, this simple recipe is bursting with delicious sweetness. You can use shop-bought coconut powder, but making your own from desiccated coconut is easy and adds a distinct freshness to the finished dessert.

125g/4½oz/1¼ cups **desiccated coconut**

100ml/3½fl oz/6½ tbsp **condensed milk**

1 PUT the desiccated coconut in a spice mill and grind to a fine powder.

2 POUR the condensed milk into a small saucepan and warm over a low heat. Add 100g/3½oz/½ cup coconut powder and simmer for 2–3 minutes, stirring constantly, until the mixture leaves the side of the pan. Watch carefully so it does not burn.

3 REMOVE the pan from the heat and set aside until the coconut mixture is just cool enough to handle.

4 SPRINKLE the remaining coconut powder onto a plate. Wet your hands and shape the mixture into 10–12 balls of equal size. Roll each ball in the coconut powder to cover them evenly. Serve immediately, or transfer to an airtight container and refrigerate for 5–6 days.

EXOTIC FRUIT SALAD

PHALON KA SALAAD

SERVES 4 PREPARATION TIME: 10 MINUTES, PLUS CHILLING TIME

Mango, the national fruit of India, is also known traditionally as the food of the gods. Its leaves are used as floral decorations during Hindu marriages and religious ceremonies. Used in all sorts of sweet preparations, mangoes are delicious eaten on their own or with other fruits, such as in this refreshing salad.

1 **papaya**

1 **mango**

1 **banana**, sliced

1 handful **strawberries**, hulled

2 tsp freshly squeezed **lime juice**

2 tsp **dark demerara** or **dark brown sugar**

1 PEEL the papaya with a knife, then cut it lengthways, scoop out and discard the seeds and cut the flesh into 2.5cm/1in pieces.

2 SLICE the mango lengthways either side of the large flat stone. Place the 2 sides flesh side up and make criss-cross cuts into the flesh without cutting through the skin. Push the skin gently to make the cubes stand out, then cut away the segments of flesh.

3 COMBINE the papaya and mango with the other ingredients in a bowl. Cover the bowl with cling film and refrigerate. Remove from the fridge about 30 minutes before serving to allow the salad to return to room temperature. Mix well before serving. This can be refrigerated, covered, for up to 2 days.

CARDAMOM ICE CREAM

ELAICHI KULFI

Traditionally made with boiled buffalo's milk, ice cream was brought to Pakistan and India by the Moghuls from Persia in the 1500s. It later found its way to the West as the result of colonization and immigration. This rich, velvety version makes a satisfying end to any meal.

½ tsp **cornflour**

2 tbsp **milk**

250ml/9fl oz/1 cup **evaporated milk**

250ml/9fl oz/1 cup **condensed milk**

200ml/7fl oz/¾ cup plus 1 tbsp **extra-thick double cream**

seeds from 3 **green cardamom pods**, crushed (*see page 14*)

1 PUT the cornflour in a small bowl and slowly stir in the milk until blended, then set aside.

2 POUR the evaporated milk into a saucepan and bring to the boil over a high heat. Add the condensed milk, double cream, cardamom seeds and the cornflour mixture to the boiling evaporated milk and continue boiling, stirring constantly, for a further 1 minute.

3 REMOVE the pan from the heat and leave the ice cream mixture to cool slightly.

4 TRANSFER the mixture to a blender or food processor, or use a hand-held mixer, and blend for 2 minutes, or until smooth.

5 POUR the mixture into a freezerproof container with a lid and freeze for at least 6 hours, or ideally overnight, until the ice cream is set. Take the ice cream out of the freezer 10–15 minutes before serving to allow it to soften slightly. Serve 2 small scoops per person.

RICE PUDDING *KHEER*

**SERVES 4   PREPARATION TIME: 10 MINUTES
COOKING TIME: 20 MINUTES**

Rice plays an integral role in Indian culture and lifestyle and is served at many Hindu festivals. On New Year's Day, sweet rice pudding is served to mark a new beginning. This creamy cardamom-spiced rice pudding is delectable hot or cold.

5 **pistachio nuts**, shelled

5 **almonds**, shelled

600ml/21½fl oz/2½ cups **whole milk**

100g/3½oz/½ cup **basmati rice**, rinsed

seeds from 4 **green cardamom pods**
(*see page 14*)

2 tbsp **sugar**

1 PUT the pistachio nuts and almonds in a heatproof bowl, pour over enough boiling water to cover and leave to soak for about 10 minutes. Drain the nuts, then use your fingers to pop them out of their skins before coarsely chopping them.

2 COMBINE the milk and rice in a saucepan over a medium heat and simmer for 12 minutes, stirring frequently so the grains do not stick on the base of the pan and the milk does not boil over.

3 RESERVE 1 teaspoon of the chopped nuts for garnishing and stir the rest of the nuts and the cardamom seeds into the rice. Simmer, stirring, for 2–3 minutes while the milk and rice bubble gently.

4 STIR in the sugar and continue to simmer, stirring, for 5–6 minutes until the sugar dissolves and the rice is tender.

5 SPOON into serving bowls or cups and sprinkle with the reserved chopped nuts, then serve at once. Alternatively, leave the pudding to cool completely, then transfer to a bowl, cover with cling film and refrigerate until required, up to 2 days. This pudding can be served chilled or at room temperature. It can be reheated once: put it in a saucepan and slowly heat 5 to 7 minutes until piping hot – add a few tablespoons of milk to prevent it becoming too thick.

MILK FUDGE *BARFI*

MAKES **16** PIECES PREPARATION TIME: **5** MINUTES, PLUS COOLING TIME
COOKING TIME: **12** MINUTES

This traditional Indian sweet made from dried or condensed milk and cooked with sugar until it solidifies can be flavoured with nuts, flour, spices — and even lentils or vegetables. The basic version here will get you started. For a spicy variation, add a pinch of cardamom while mixing. Serve small squares of this fudge with afternoon tea or coffee, or at the end of a meal.

1 tsp **butter**

55g/2oz/¼ cup **caster sugar**

185ml/6fl oz/¾ cup **double cream**

125g/4½oz full-fat **milk powder**

1 MELT the butter in a heavy-based saucepan over a medium heat. Add the sugar and cook, stirring continuously, for 3 minutes, until the sugar melts.

2 ADD the cream and simmer, stirring occasionally, for 3 minutes.

3 TIP in the milk powder and continue simmering, stirring, for 5 minutes, or until the mixture becomes stiff and begins to leave the side of the pan.

4 POUR the mixture onto a sheet of greaseproof paper and leave it to stand for a couple of minutes, then use a wet palette knife or spatula to shape it into a 10cm/4in square about 1.5cm/¾in thick.

5 LEAVE the mixture to cool completely. Using a sharp knife, cut the cooled fudge into sixteen 2.5cm/1in squares. Serve immediately with coffee, or transfer to an airtight container and refrigerate for up to 5 days.

SEMOLINA PUDDING *SHEERA*

SERVES 4   PREPARATION TIME: 5 MINUTES   COOKING TIME: 7 MINUTES

This dessert is served during religious festivals, such as Diwali, the Hindu festival of lights. A quick and simple comforting pudding, it can be prepared in just a few minutes, just before serving.

60g/2¼oz **butter**

85g/3oz/⅔ cup **fine semolina**

55g/2oz/¼ cup **sugar**

4 tbsp **double cream**

1 **banana**, sliced

6 shelled **pistachio nuts**, chopped

seeds from 2 **green cardamom pods**
   (see page 14)

1 BRING 200ml/7fl oz/scant 1 cup water to the boil. Melt the butter in a saucepan over a medium heat. Add the semolina and cook for 5 minutes, stirring constantly, or until the mixture becomes clumpy, light sand in colour and has a toasty aroma.

2 POUR over the boiling water, add the sugar and cream and stir until the sugar dissolves.

3 STIR in the banana, pistachio nuts and cardamom seeds. Serve warm.

CREAMY YOGURT DESSERT

SHRIKHAND

Strained yogurt has a decadently rich and creamy texture – for the best results, use full-fat yogurt. This dish from western Indian often features fruits, nuts and spices and is sometimes served alongside deep-fried breads.

500g/1lb 2oz **natural yogurt**

seeds from 5 **green cardamom pods** (*see page 14*)

2 tbsp **icing sugar**

6 **saffron strands**

15 **pistachio nuts**, shelled and crushed or chopped

1 **PUT** the yogurt in a large fine-mesh nylon sieve. Place the sieve over a bowl, cover and refrigerate for at least 8 hours, or overnight, to allow the whey, or excess liquid, to drain away.

2 **GRIND** the cardamom seeds to a powder with a pestle and mortar.

3 **PLACE** the yogurt, ground cardamom seeds, sugar and saffron strands in a bowl and mix well.

4 **STIR** in the nuts, cover the bowl with cling film and chill in the fridge until ready to serve. Serve with hot Pooris (see page 30).

MANGO YOGURT DRINK

AAM KA LASSI

SERVES 4   PREPARATION TIME: 5 MINUTES

Popular during the hot summer months, particularly in northern India, this refreshing beverage is made by blending yogurt and spices. Savoury versions may be seasoned with cumin and black pepper, but this classic sweet variation uses mango pulp. The Alphonso mango, one of the sweetest in the world, yields the tastiest result. If fresh mangoes are not available, you can buy mango pulp in cans from many supermarkets and most Asian food shops.

seeds from 2 **green cardamom pods**
(*see page 14*)

4 large ripe **mangoes**, peeled and chopped
(*see page 18*)

500ml/17fl oz/2 cups **natural yogurt**

500ml/17fl oz/2 cups **milk**

4 tsp **caster sugar**

ice, to serve

1 GRIND the cardamom seeds to a powder with a pestle and mortar.

2 PUT the chopped mangoes in a blender and blend until a smooth pulp forms. This should yield about 500ml/17fl oz/2 cups mango pulp.

3 ADD the ground cardamom seeds, yogurt, milk and sugar to the blender and blend until smooth. Alternatively, whisk all the ingredients together in a large bowl.

4 SERVE at once, over ice, in tall glasses.

SPICY TEA _MASALA CHAI_

Fragrant cinnamon, cardamom, clove and fennel combine to create a delightfully spicy tea. In India, teas are defined by the regions in which they are grown, hence the names Darjeeling, Assam and Nilgiri – so experiment with different varieties to find the one you like best.

5cm/2in piece **cassia bark** or **cinnamon stick**

2 **green cardamom pods**, lightly crushed

2 **cloves**

1 tsp **fennel seeds**

2 tsp **tea leaves**

4 tsp **sugar** (optional)

250ml/9fl oz/1 cup **milk**

1 BOIL 500ml/17fl oz/2 cups water in a saucepan over a high heat. Add the cassia bark or cinnamon, cardamom pods, cloves and fennel seeds and continue boiling for 2 minutes.

2 ADD the tea leaves and sugar, if using, reduce the heat to low and simmer for 1 minute.

3 POUR in the milk and continue simmering for 2 minutes.

4 STRAIN the tea into teacups or mugs and serve at once.

PART 3

THE MENUS

Indian meals are informal and **friendly** affairs where the guests (even unexpected ones) are **welcomed** with open arms. Unlike Western meals that are often divided into multiple **courses**, Indian meals consist of several dishes all served at once, with the main dish usually being a particularly **elaborate** preparation. The full spectrum of **flavours**, from cool, rich and mild to spicy, hot, pungent and sweet, is also part of the **meal**. Rice or bread (or both) are indispensable staples.

This **relaxed** approach means the possibilities for combining starters, side dishes, condiments and main dishes are nearly **limitless**. The menus here are only **guides** to what an Indian host or hostess might serve for specific occasions. Once you have selected one, make sure to read through the individual **recipes**, compile a shopping list and then review the **easy-to-follow** timeline so that preparing your menu is as **peaceful** and stress-free as possible.

Once you have got the hang of following the menus, feel free to **mix** and match some of your favourite recipes from this book to **create** new menus to share with your friends and **family**.

SIMPLE LUNCH

This simple lunch suggestion offers all the flavours of India in one go. It is not too spicy for lunchtime but has all the components to make a balanced Indian meal with different colours and textures.

SWEET POTATO CURRY
(see page 75)

CHICKEN JALFREZI
(see page 96)

CARROT SALAD
(see page 163)

CORIANDER CHUTNEY
(see page 19)

PLAIN BASMATI RICE
(see page 31)

Halve all the recipe ingredients if you are preparing a meal for two people. The coriander chutney and the paste for the chicken dish can be made the night before. The onions, garlic and chillies for the chicken and the vegetables for the carrot salad can also be chopped and stored in an airtight container overnight.

PM
12.30 COOK the chicken dish, then set aside and leave to cool.
1.00 PEEL, chop and boil the sweet potatoes. Drain well and set aside.
1.15 SEASON the carrot salad ingredients while the potatoes are boiling, then set aside to serve at room temperature.
1.30 CHOP the chilli for the sweet potato dish and fry it with the cumin seeds, then finish cooking the potato dish. Cover and keep warm.
1.45 COOK the rice just before serving, so that it will be piping hot.
1.50 REHEAT the chicken in the saucepan over a medium-low heat. Quickly reheat the sweet potatoes as well, if necessary, while the chicken reheats.
2.00 SERVE the Sweet Potato Curry, Chicken Jalfrezi and Plain Basmati Rice hot, with the Carrot Salad and Coriander Chutney.

PREPARATION NOTES
Save time by using CHILLI POWDER instead of green chillies for the chicken dish, if you like. The difference in flavour will be subtle, and the final result will be just as delicious.

LUNCH BOX

TANDOORI CHICKEN BITES
(see page 51)

CUMIN-INFUSED PEAS
(see page 148)

SPICED RICE
(see page 32)

MANGO CHUTNEY
(see page 19)

TIME PLAN

All the dishes in this menu can be prepared the day before and make an enjoyable change from cold sushi or sandwiches. The menu avoids gravy-based dishes, so there is no danger of spillages in your bag.

All the recipes serve four, so you will need to adjust the quantities to suit your needs: halve the recipes if preparing only two lunch boxes, or quarter them if you are preparing only one. The day or evening before, marinate and grill the chicken bites, then leave them to cool completely and store, covered, in the fridge overnight. Also, make the pea dish the night before, cool completely and refrigerate in a sealed container. The rice dish is best made fresh in the morning, but you can also make it the night before if you prefer. The chutney can be prepared a few days in advance and stored in the fridge.

AM 7.15 **COOK** the rice and leave to cool. Make sure it is completely cool before you pack it for transporting.

7.50 **PACK** the Tandoori Chicken Bites, the Cumin-infused Peas and the Spiced Rice in one container and the Mango Chutney in a separate sealed container.

PREPARATION NOTES

For extra flavour sprinkle some **CORIANDER LEAVES** over the chicken, rice and peas before packing them. You can **TRANSFORM** leftover Tandoori Chicken Bites into Chicken Tikka Masala (see page 84) for an evening meal and store any leftover mango chutney in the fridge — it keeps up to 2 weeks.

MID-WEEK LUNCH WITH FAMILY

Simple and mild dishes with a hint of chilli heat and spice make up this quick and easy lunch menu for four. The chicken dish doesn't contain too much spice and is softened by the coconut and nuts in the gravy. It is like having a takeaway from your favourite Indian restaurant, only nicer. The lentils provide a balance to the creamy chicken – a hearty recipe for all the family.

TOMATO, ONION AND CHILLI SALAD

(see page 160)

CREAMY CHICKEN CURRY

(see page 99)

TEMPERED RED LENTILS

(see page 143)

NAANS

(see page 26)

Boil the red lentils the night before until they become mushy, but don't add the spices for the tempering. The naans can also be made ahead and then reheated before serving, but in Indian households they are always made fresh.

11.00 AM	**MAKE** and knead the naan dough, then cover the bowl and leave the dough to rise in a warm place.
12.00 PM	**COOK** the chicken curry, but do not add the ginger or garam masala, then set aside to cool completely.
12.30	**MAKE** the salad, then cover and chill.
12.45	**PREHEAT** the oven to 200°C/400°F/Gas 6 and grease a baking tray.
12.50	**SHAPE** and bake the naans. Wrap them in a clean tea towel to keep warm if they are finished baking before the other dishes are reheated.
1:15	**REHEAT** the chicken curry, stirring in the ginger and garam masala.
1:25	**REHEAT** the lentils and fry the curry leaves and other spices for tempering, then add the buttery spice mixture into the lentils, stir well and finish cooking.
1:30	**SERVE** the Creamy Chicken Curry, Tempered Red Lentils and Naans hot, with the chilled Tomato, Onion and Chilli Salad.

PREPARATION NOTES

For **VARIETY** use split yellow lentils instead of red. The exact cooking time depends on how old they are – older lentils take longer. If the **GRAVY** seems dry when reheating the chicken, stir in some water and watch carefully so it does not burn.

MID-WEEK LUNCH WITH FRIENDS

SPICED WHITE FISH COOKED IN COCONUT

(see page 127)

SPICED BLACK-EYED BEANS

(see page 144)

FENUGREEK FLATBREADS

(see page 28)

SEMOLINA PUDDING

(see page 180)

PREPARATION NOTES

FRESH FISH should smell like the sea – not "fishy". The eyes should be clear and the gills bright red when purchased. In southern India this fish dish is traditionally made with seer fish, a type of **MACKEREL**. So, if you prefer, you can substitute the sole specified in the recipe with mackerel.

TIME PLAN

The fresh flavours of the southern Indian-style fish dish in this menu complement the nuttiness of the black-eyed beans and the fenugreek-spiced flatbreads. The semolina pudding is a gorgeous comfort dessert that is reassuringly filling and satisfying.

All the recipes in this menu are so quick and simple, they can be made on the day of the lunch, before your friends arrive.

12.00 PM   **MAKE** the semolina pudding. Leave it to cool completely and then cover and set aside.

12.35   **POUR** boiling water over the tamarind pulp in the fish recipe to extract the seeds and fibres. Mix the tamarind juice with the spices and boiling water in the recipe and set aside.

12.45   **COOK** the spiced beans but do not add the ginger and coriander leaves at the end of the recipe, then set aside.

1.00   **MIX** and knead the dough for the flatbreads, then cover the bowl and leave to rest.

1.15   **COOK** the spiced fish dish and keep it warm over a low heat, without boiling.

1.25   **REHEAT** the spiced beans until hot, Sprinkle them with the ginger and coriander, cover and keep warm.

1.30   **SHAPE** and cook the flatbreads just before serving.

1.45   **SERVE** the Spiced White Fish Cooked in Coconut, Spiced Black-Eyed Beans and Fenugreek Flatbreads hot.

2.15   **REHEAT** the Semolina Pudding. If it has become too thick, add 4 tablespoons water and stir until smooth and heated through. Serve warm.

WEEKEND LUNCH WITH FAMILY

CHICKEN TIKKA MASALA
(see page 84)

BUTTERY SPINACH AND POTATOES
(see page 71)

PULAO RICE WITH PEAS
(see page 32)

CARDAMOM ICE CREAM
(see page 175)

PREPARATION NOTES

Indian ICE CREAM is denser than Western ice creams, so remember to take it out of the freezer so it can soften in time. For an authentic touch, freeze the ice cream in TRADITIONAL conical-shaped moulds sold in Indian food shops.

TIME PLAN

Using mostly humble ingredients, this relaxing, well-deserved weekend menu features the robust, warming flavours of northern Indian cuisine. It is an ideal, comforting choice after a long week.

Marinate the Tandoori Chicken Bites (see page 51) for the chicken recipe the evening before or the morning of the lunch. The ice cream is a handy, standby dessert to have in the freezer, as it can be made up to three months in advance. If you want to get even more of a head start, cook the rice in the morning and reheat it just before serving.

11.55 AM   CUT the potatoes and rinse the spinach, then prepare the remaining ingredients for the potato recipe and set aside.

12.15 PM   ASSEMBLE the ingredients for the chicken dish and set aside. Rinse the rice, assemble the spices it is cooked with it, chop the chilli and then set aside.

1.00   COOK the chicken dish, then set aside for reheating just before serving. Preheat the oven to 160°C/325°F/Gas 3.

1.15   COOK the spinach and potatoes and keep them warm, covered with foil, in the oven until ready to serve.

1.55   COOK the rice with the peas, then cover and keep hot.

2.10   REHEAT the chicken dish over a medium-low heat, stirring occasionally, for 7–9 minutes until hot, but not boiling.

2.20   SERVE the Chicken Tikka Masala, Buttery Spinach and Potatoes, and Pulao Rice with Peas hot.

2.40   TRANSFER the ice cream to the fridge to soften.

2.55   SCOOP the Cardamom Ice Cream into bowls and serve.

WEEKEND LUNCH WITH FRIENDS

CABBAGE WITH RED CHILLIES

(see page 155)

MALABAR KING PRAWN CURRY

(see page 132)

MAHARASHTRIAN LENTILS

(see page 140)

PLAIN BASMATI RICE

(see page 31)

CASHEW NUT DIAMONDS

(see page 168)

PREPARATION NOTES

The LENTIL dish is best eaten the day it is made, so don't prepare it the evening before. The spices are most flavourful when added just before serving.

TIME PLAN

Just a few striking ingredients make up this simple yet exotic menu that offers maximum flavour with minimum effort or skill. The earthiness of the Plain Basmati Rice compliments the aromatic dishes of this delicious spread.

A day or two before, make the cashew nut dessert, transfer it to an airtight container and refrigerate. Make the lentils in the morning, but don't add the spices. The prawn curry is best cooked right before serving minute but if you are worried about time it can be made in the morning and reheated with an extra 4 tablespoons water stirred in.

PM
12.00 PREPARE and assemble all the ingredients for the prawn curry and set aside. Rinse the rice and set aside.

12.40 PREHEAT the oven to 160°C/325°F/Gas 3. Cook the cabbage dish until the cabbage is just tender, then transfer to an ovenproof serving dish, cover with foil and leave in the oven until ready to serve. Take care not to overcook the cabbage.

12.55 PREPARE and cook the lentils, through the point where you add the boiling water, then set aside for reheating just before serving.

1.00 MAKE the prawn curry and keep it warm.

1.20 COOK the rice. Reheat the lentils, mashing them against the side of the pan, then leave to simmer while the rice cooks.

1.30 SERVE the Cabbage with Red Chillies, Malabar King Prawn Curry, Maharashtrian Lentils and Plain Basmati Rice hot in separate serving dishes in the centre of the table for everyone to help themselves.

2.15 ARRANGE the Cashew Nut Diamonds on a plate (as you would a plate of biscuits) and invite your guests to nibble on them while they drink tea, coffee or dessert wine.

SIMPLE DINNER

The contrasting colours and diversity of flavours in these dishes make a simple yet delightful meal. The creamy and comforting chicken combined with the lightly spiced spring greens, tangy tomato relish and turmeric-infused rice make this an all-round pleaser.

BUTTER CHICKEN
(see page 88)

SPICED SPRING GREENS
(see page 156)

TURMERIC RICE
(see page 33)

TOMATO CHUTNEY
(see page 21)

Halve all the recipe ingredients if you are preparing dinner for two. Marinate the chicken the night before, then cover and place in the fridge. The chutney can be made any time up to two weeks in advance and stored in a sealed jar.

PM

6.45 PREPARE the ingredients for the Butter Chicken sauce, stopping after step 4. Remove the pan from the heat and set aside.

7.00 PREPARE all the ingredients for the spring greens dish. Rinse the rice and set aside. Remove the chicken pieces from the fridge.

7.30 FRY the spices for the rice, then complete the recipe.

7.40 REHEAT the sauce for the chicken over a medium heat, then reduce the heat to low, add the butter and chicken pieces to the sauce and simmer until the chicken is cooked through.

7.50 FRY the spring greens.

8.00 SERVE the Butter Chicken, Spiced Spring Greens and Turmeric Rice hot. Put the Tomato Chutney in a small, non-metallic dish or ramekin and serve.

PREPARATION NOTES

Use **KALE** or **SWISS CHARD** instead of spring greens. It is best to buy the greens on the day or the day before, no earlier. Choose greens with firm, uniform-coloured leaves that are not wilted or discoloured. Rinse them thoroughly before cooking to remove the sandy grit.

ROMANTIC DINNER

PREPARATION NOTES

HALIBUT is a large, mild, white flatfish. It is available in steaks, cutlets or fillets. The firm, meaty flesh has a subtle flavour and complements sauces wonderfully. The fruit salad can be made up to two days ahead if you want to **SAVE TIME**, but the flavours really are best when it is made fresh.

TIME PLAN

This menu balances a number of lively flavours, striking colours, tantalizing textures and fragrant aromas to create a memorable dining experience.

To prepare this meal for two people, halve all the recipe quantities. Make the coriander paste in step 3 of the halibut recipe the night before the dinner, then refrigerate in an airtight container until ready to use.

6.45 PM **PREPARE** the ingredients for the green pepper dish and set aside. Rinse the rice and set aside. Soak the tamarind pulp and prepare the remaining ingredients for the halibut dish.

7.10 **CHOP** the papaya and mango for the salad, then slice the banana and hull the strawberries. Place all the fruit in a serving bowl and add the lime juice and sugar, then cover and refrigerate.

7.25 **SOAK** the saffron strands and fry the spices for the rice dish, then continue with the recipe, cooking the rice until it is fluffy.

7.35 **MAKE** the halibut dish, while the rice is cooking. Be careful not to break up the fish pieces.

7.45 **FRY** the garlic and onion for the green pepper dish, then complete the dish while the halibut is cooking.

7.55 **REMOVE** the fruit salad from the refrigerator.

8.00 **SERVE** the Halibut with Green Chilies and Cilantro, Green Peppers with Cumin, and Saffron Rice hot, followed by the Exotic Fruit Salad at room temperature.

MID-WEEK DINNER WITH FAMILY

GRIDDLED CHICKEN

(see page 95)

MIXED VEGETABLE CURRY

(see page 76)

KIDNEY BEANS IN SPICY TOMATO AND GARLIC GRAVY

(see page 67)

BALTI POTATOES

(see page 139)

EXOTIC LEAVENED NAANS

(see page 27)

PREPARATION NOTES

If any vegetable in the curry isn't to your family's liking, try substituting it with **GREEN BEANS** or **COURGETTE**. Add them along with the broccoli and red pepper to ensure they are tender before adding them to the masala.

TIME PLAN

From the quick, flash-fry chicken dish to the warming kidney bean curry and the freshness of the herbs in the mixed vegetables, this relaxed, informal menu is a perfect treat for a family with a hectic schedule. The recipes are not too chilli-hot, so everyone will enjoy them.

Make the naans the night before and store in an airtight container. Cook the kidney bean dish too so the flavours have time to develop, but do not add the final seasoning of salt and garam masala or the coriander leaves. You can also make the masala paste for the vegetable curry and store it in the fridge.

PM
5.50 PEEL, chop and boil the potatoes for the balti dish. While the potatoes are boiling, make the coarse paste that flavours the dish.
6.05 FINISH cooking the potato dish, then set aside in the pan.
6.35 COOK the vegetable curry, using the masala paste prepared the night before. Set aside in the pan, ready for reheating.
7.00 PREPARE the Griddled Chicken, cooking until just before the fresh fenugreek leaves are added. Cover and set aside until serving. Preheat the oven to 180°C/350°F/Gas 4.
7.40 REHEAT the kidney beans until hot. Stir in the salt and garam masala, transfer to a serving bowl and sprinkle with coriander leaves. While the beans are heating, finish the chicken dish and keep it hot in the oven.
7.45 SPRINKLE the naans with a little water, wrap in foil and place in the oven to reheat.
7.55 REHEAT the potatoes.
8.00 SERVE the Griddled Chicken, Mixed Vegetable Curry, Kidney Beans in Spicy Tomato and Garlic Gravy, Balti Potatoes and Exotic Leavened Naans hot.

MID-WEEK DINNER WITH FRIENDS

TIME PLAN

The various fresh herbs, whole spices and spice blends used in these recipes make this an unforgettable meal to savour. The refreshing, spiced fresh tomato soup seasons the palate for the dishes to follow, which combines North Indian cooking with Goanese tastes and aromas.

The day before, marinate the pork for the vindaloo dish and make the soup, then store everything in the fridge. Leave the yogurt for the dessert to strain overnight.

PM
6.00 PREPARE all the ingredients for the green bean dish and the chickpea curry and set aside. There are a lot of ingredients so make sure you have everything ready before you start cooking.

6.15 FINISH preparing the yogurt dessert, then cover and refrigerate.

6.20 REMOVE the marinated pork from the fridge. Rinse the basmati rice and set aside.

6.25 COOK the green bean recipe until the beans are not quite tender, then set aside in the same pan for reheating.

6.40 TRANSFER the marinated pork to a saucepan and finish cooking.

6.55 BREW the tea for the chickpeas, finish the recipe and set aside.

7.30 COOK the rice. Just before the rice finishes cooking, quickly reheat the green beans over a high heat, stirring. At the same time, reheat the chickpea curry over a medium-high heat until hot.

7.45 REMOVE the soup from the fridge, put it in a saucepan and reheat, then ladle into bowls. Serve the soup hot, as a separate first course, or Indian-style along with the other dishes.

7.55 TRANSFER the rice to a large serving bowl.

8.00 SERVE the Tomato Soup, Pork Vindaloo, Chickpea Curry, Green Beans with Garlic and Mustard Seeds and Plain Basmati Rice hot.

8.45 SERVE the chilled Creamy Yogurt Dessert.

DINNER PARTY

TIME PLAN

This stunning dinner party line-up takes you and your guests on a tasting tour of India. Spicy, mild, sweet and pungent flavours all abound, and though the menu may look elaborate, many of the dishes can be prepared the day before – so you get to enjoy the party too.

To serve eight people, double all the recipes. The day before, cook the chicken dish, the basmati rice for the biryani and the prawn mixture for the pooris, then make the dessert. Store in the fridge overnight.

PM

2.30 MAKE the garam masala and prepare the remaining ingredients for the biryani. Prepare the ingredients for the paneer and fish dishes.

2.50 COOK the lamb for the biryani and leave to cool.

3.00 MAKE the dough for the pooris, then knead, shape, roll out and fry.

4.00 COOK the fish curry, then leave to cool completely, cover and chill.

4.30 COOK the paneer dish, but do not add the ginger, cream, garam masala or coriander, then set aside to cool.

5.30 ASSEMBLE the layers of lamb and rice for the biryani. Cover the casserole and put in the fridge until required.

7.00 PREHEAT the oven to 180°C/350°F/Gas 4 for cooking the biryani and reheating the pooris. Remove the biryani from the fridge.

7.25 PUT the biryani in the oven.

7.45 REHEAT the prawn mixture, the fish curry and the chicken in separate pans over a low heat, stirring occasionally, then cover tightly.

7.50 REHEAT the pooris in the oven while the biryani finishes cooking.

7.55 ASSEMBLE the Prawn Pooris and remove the biryani from the oven. Reheat the paneer, then stir in the ginger and cream and sprinkle with garam masala and coriander.

8.00 SERVE the Prawn Pooris hot, as a first course, then serve the other hot dishes together and round off the meal with the Coconut Treats.

DRINKS PARTY

TIME PLAN

Fantastic flavours for all tastes make up this drinks party menu. These dishes, generous bite-sized portions of popular starters, are more than just nibbles. Arrange small portions of each item on serving plates and refill as needed. This menu will cater for six to eight guests.

The night before, marinate the minced lamb for the kebabs, then mould the meat around the metal skewers, cover and refrigerate. Make and assemble the samosas, then cover and refrigerate. The chutneys and relishes should also be made the day before.

PM
5.15 MAKE the batter mixtures for the Onion Fritters, Deep-fried Fish and Prawn Fritters. Cover and set each aside in a separate bowl.

6.10 PREHEAT the grill to medium. Remove the samosas and fish from the fridge. Preheat the oven to 160°C/325°F/Gas 3.

6.15 GRILL the lamb kebabs, then wrap in foil and place in the oven.

6.30 HEAT the oil for deep-frying the samosas to 190°C/375°F.

6.35 DEEP-FRY the samosas in batches, then drain on kitchen paper. When they are all fried, wrap them in foil and keep them warm in the oven. Reheat the oil and deep-fry the onion fritters, then put them in the oven to keep warm.

7.00 PUT a fresh batch of oil in the fryer and reheat to 190°C/375°F. Fry the prawn fritters and drain on kitchen paper.

7.15 REMOVE everything from the oven and arrange on serving plates.

7.30 SERVE all the starters hot, with the chilled chutneys and relishes, buffet style for your guests to help themselves, or arrange small portions of each item on serving plates, as shown, then pass them around and refill the plates as needed.

INDEX